The First Arab Spring: Reclaiming the Sermon on the Mount as a Radical Movement of Political and Spiritual Change

© 2019 Jarrod Cochran

This edition © 2019 Radical Left Media (Atlanta)
ISBN: 9781726273534

Library of Congress Cataloging-in-Publication Data
Published in the United States of America

The First Arab Spring

Reclaiming the Sermon on the Mount as a Radical

Movement

of Political and Spiritual Change

by

Rev. Dr. Jarrod Cochran

For Stephanie and Owen.

You truly taught me that God is love and that love is indeed radical.

"We need in every bay and community a group of angelic troublemakers."

-   Bayard Rustin

TABLE OF CONTENTS

INTRODUCTION

Politics. This word brings discomfort to many. From the cringe-worthy thoughts of the family member uttering some nonsensical political talking-point s/he heard from on Fox News during a holiday dinner to your liberal friend talking about the racism of the Republican Party while quickly locking the door of their car when they see a person of color walking by; it is little wonder why this topic causes anxiety for so many. Perhaps even in spite of these routine scenarios, politics are unavoidable, as it molds and shapes the society we live in and the world at large.

Politics, specifically how to maneuver politics to greater represent the poor and oppressed, have intrigued me since I was a young adult. Now, I've never been good at sports nor had much interest in them, (ask any friend or family member for verification), so the political arena became my "game" of choice; studying Political Science, memorizing the "rosters" for all the major and minor "teams", and watching with great interest all of their "championship matches" (read: debates and elections). Spectating has never been enough for me, either. Involving myself in protests, grassroots activism, and regularly confronting lawmakers is part of the process. Before embracing anarchism,[1] I wanted to join the political ranks as a state senator. So, it's no coincidence that as a minister and an anarchist that the message of Jesus resonates with me in a spiritual and political way. But I also think that this was the actual intent of Jesus' message and movement. After all, what good is your faith if you're not willing to act on it?

In the midst of politicians, ministers, and countless Christians who claim Jesus is their friend and would support war, creating an ever-widening gap between the rich and the poor, sustaining inequality between genders, races, and sexual orientations, I want to offer a counter-narrative. I can think of no better place to reveal what the Jesus of the gospels *actually supported* than looking to the Sermon on the Mount. Most likely, your encounter with Jesus' Sermon on the Mount has been at church. These timid readings of

---

[1] For those of you new to this term, when I say anarchism or anarchy I'm not talking about "let's create chaos and destroy lives." Our current system of government has the monopoly on chaos and destruction of lives. No, I'm speaking of anarchism as in building actual non-hierarchal community where we share what we have with one another, care for one another, and don't have an oppressive authority hindering our rights or our abilities to live free and compassionate lives.

Jesus' sermon, which might as well be called *The Platitudes on the Mount*, leave the audience confused yet warm and fuzzy over the calm, kind words of Jesus that challenge us just a little bit (like that teacher who urged us to apply ourselves just a little harder to get a solid "B" in class). The confusion of the audience is usually due to the presenter being confused of the message, as well. What a confusing message this sermon must be indeed when we have yet to remove the shackles of our nationalistic and imperialist indoctrination that stands for everything that Jesus challenges in his message.

Instead of confusion and banality, what you will encounter in these pages is a Jesus who is snarky, bold, angry, passionate, and funny. This meeting with Jesus' great sermon will hopefully challenge you, shake you from your slumber, and cause you to think deeply about who you truly give your allegiance to. As you read further, you will find that Jesus was calling us to a revolution.

"Revolution? Political Movements? This isn't what Jesus was about," I can hear some of you (probably from my childhood church) exclaiming. If this movement that Jesus was creating was not one of political reckoning, what would be the point of his message or work? Staunch traditionalist Christians will argue that the point of Jesus was to die as a sacrifice for the sins of humanity.[2] However, if this were the whole point of Jesus, would not the gospels begin and end with his crucifixion? If Jesus' death was the only note of importance, why dedicate four gospels, (not including the countless ones left out of our biblical canon), to the teachings and message of Jesus? If Jesus' message was not a political one that had powerful momentum, what then would cause the authorities and priests to fear the people?[3] Jesus' message was having a true impact with the oppressed peoples of his land – so much that it was creating palpable pressure on the powers and authorities.

May what follows inspire you to continue Jesus' work of love, grace, and radical opposition to the status quo. After all, either

---

[2] This ugly idea of substitutionary atonement was not widely embraced or believed until the 11th Century with Anslem of Canterbury's treatise *Cur Deus Homo*. Before Anslem solidified the idea of Jesus' death being a transaction between God and humanity's sins, the Early Christians actually saw Jesus' death and sacrifice as something different entirely. The Early Christians saw Jesus' death and resurrection as *Christus Victor*. Jesus' victory over death, the devil, and all the powers and principalities that held people in bondage. This is why the earliest readings of the Apostle's Creed describe Jesus descending into Hell and breaking the gates wide open to rescue the souls there.

[3] Mark 11:32

we're Christians who are dedicated enough to take Jesus' words seriously about standing up for the poor and oppressed, or we need to stop wasting our time and following someone that we disagree on the most basic of levels.

1
<u>WHY WE NEED A POLITICAL JESUS</u>

Before we go further, we need to ask, *"what if?"* What if Jesus actually *meant* the things he said? What if all of those teachings on God's kingdom, of loving your enemies, of caring for the "least of these"... *what if* instead of coming up with reasons why these teachings should be relegated to another time or passed off as lofty ideals... *what if* Jesus actually meant for us to follow them?

I remember attending an evangelical mega church in North Georgia during the beginning of the second Iraq War in 2003. This, of course, became quite the topic of discussion within the church groups. So much so that one of the ministers came up to the stage one Sunday morning and made this statement:

> "I look out in our parking lot and notice a
> lot of people have bumper stickers in
> support of the Iraq War. I also noticed that
> there are a few of you with bumper stickers

against it. I have also noticed that this has become a frequent topic in our church. This needs to stop. The thing is: we're over there fighting for justice, so we should quit talking about it."

How have we as a Church, the followers of the Prince of Peace, come to a point where we are divided over issues like war and unchecked violence? Furthermore, how have we as a Church come to a point where a pastor demands that those who question the actions of a government or empire remain silent? Our modern Church is akin to one's reflection in a funhouse mirror. The ideas, teachings, and beliefs of Jesus - all found in the gospels - are distorted and perverted to the point that we dare make rationalizations for war and capital punishment. We see no problem in tying scripture to our support for the State and its policies - regardless of who it harms. We easily create justifications for why we should refuse to help the poor, and even go so far as to move out of their neighborhoods and into more affluent locations.

So again, the question must be asked: How have we, as the Church, come to this point?

It is my conviction that we have found ourselves in this place because we have failed to take the words of Jesus seriously. We have removed from Jesus' message its radical implications. We have filed down the teeth and we have sanded down the nails of the Lion of Judah – the one who called on his followers to proclaim an allegiance to God's kingdom over any earthly empire. Why? So that we could make his message more palatable and more domesticated? We have twisted Jesus' words. Instead of learning of Jesus teaching his followers to respond to the powers of this world, we have turned his teachings into mere platitudes and anecdotes on how to get to heaven and how to be good, moral, obedient citizens of whatever kingdom, empire, or government we find ourselves in. While this may be the Jesus we find in most of our modern Churches, this is *not* the Jesus we encounter in the holy texts.

Jesus commanded his followers to relinquish any and all forms of power and glory. When referring to God's kingdom, Jesus was not merely talking about, as Dr. Dallas Willard puts it, "a feathery and ethereal realm,"[4] removed and separated from the world around us. Jesus was speaking to us about a divine "kingdom" here on earth.[5] God's kingdom, according to Jesus, is to be established and furthered through radical political action, inspired and infused by faith in God and God's goodness. This kingdom of God is to remove any and every distinction of wealth and status; any "power" that allows individuals to demand the subservience/obedience of others. Love is the key and the over-arching law of God's new kingdom.

The evidence of Jesus building a spiritual and political movement based on this law of love is throughout the gospels. In the beginning of Jesus' ministry, we see that Jesus preached this kingdom manifesto mostly in parable. To openly speak of God's kingdom would demand that both the Roman Empire and the Temple priesthood of Judaism should be overthrown. However, as Jesus' following grew, so too did his boldness. Jesus began speaking openly of God's kingdom, despite that fact that he knew an "anti-

---

[4] Dallas Willard, *The Divine Conspiracy: Rediscovering our Hidden Life in God* (New York: Harper Collins, 1998), 12.

[5] Not to be confused with creating a literal theocracy. When Jesus spoke of God's kingdom on the earth, he was insisting that we behave ourselves as if we are citizens of that kingdom.

establishment" message would make him a target. This boldness even led to lampooning Governor Pontius Pilate's grand entrance into Jerusalem during Jewish Passover - which included a battalion of Roman soldiers and powerful steeds - by riding into town on the back of a donkey and openly debating the priests at the Temple. He even created street-theater by *occupying* the Temple, overturning the money-changers' tables and driving their wares out into the city street. The boldness and the directness of Jesus' vision of God's kingdom is what, I contend, eventually found him nailed to a Roman cross between two thieves and labeled as an insurrectionist.

Indeed, Jesus preached revolution – a *real* revolution – not merely a spiritual transformation. He believed in combining a political revolution with a spiritual end, revealing how to bring God down from heaven, out of the pages of the holy texts, and into our own world. Professor and author, Stanley Hauerwas, states this very thing: "Having challenged the notion that Christianity is fundamentally a system of belief...we want to argue that Christianity is mostly a matter of politics - politics as defined by the gospel. The call to be part of the gospel is a joyful call to be adopted by an alien people, to join a counter-cultural phenomenon, a new *polls* called church."[6]

This radical and subversive understanding of Jesus' message is desperately needed this country. Let's not kid ourselves, the United States of America has embraced racism, xenophobia, and genocide since it's inception. Our nation's history is settled on the mounds of countless murdered Native Americans and its edifices built on the backs of slave labor. We've never known a time of peace as the United States has exited military wars so that they could jump into another. Our runaway capitalism has incurred countless victims who were slaughtered like wicked sacrifices for the few elite to maintain power and wealth. Our nation's diseases of racism, hatred, violence, toxic masculinity, and misogyny have metastasized, bursting forth their illnesses to the surface in the forms of President Donald Trump and overt white supremacy. We should have sought healing and a cure when these symptoms presented themselves as the toxin known as neo-liberalism through the presidential runs of Reagan, Bush I and II, Clinton, and Obama.

---

[6] Stanley Hauerwas, *Resident Aliens: Life in the Christian Colony* (Nashville: Abingdon Press, 1989), 6.

It is in this backdrop of police brutality, late-stage capitalism, ecocide, systemic oppression of the poor and minorities, multiple wars and the threat of nuclear war, the re-energizing of white supremacist and fascist groups, the slaughter of children in schools, and the transformation of the American Church into a nationalist death cult that we need to rediscover Jesus' radical message and subversive politics. It is in this stage that it is incumbent upon us to read Jesus' Sermon on the Mount with fresh eyes.

2
<u>JESUS' POLITICAL PLATFORM</u>

I remember studying the Beatitudes, in Sunday School at my childhood church. Well, perhaps "studying" is not the correct term. In our church, where the American flag hung just a little bit higher than the Christian flag, I would say that instead of studying these verses we would stare at them in utter bewilderment. None can explain the meaning of these verses without first abandoning the deeply held and false conviction that the United States Constitution and the platform of the Republican Party hold the same moral wisdom as the words of Jesus of Nazareth. This discarding of nationalistic ideals, however, was not an exercise our teachers nor us fearful students were willing to partake in.

If only we would have taken that leap of faith, we might have realized that with these declarations, Jesus was laying out the guidelines for citizens in God's *un*kingdom.[7] These are more than

---

[7] Mark Van Steenwyk, *The Unkingdom of God: Embracing the Subversive Power of Repentance* (Downers Grove: IVP, 2003). The term unkingdom will be used throughout this book. The reason is due to the fact that when we think of the word "kingdom", the thoughts of power through military might, dominance over others, and a caste system immediately come to mind. These images should never be used to describe the realm of God, thus "unkingdom".

just mere platitudes or "nice words that should be relegated to a future time," as some Christians believe. In these verses, Jesus is revealing the building blocks for which the basis of a new society should find as correct qualities of character. It is as author Dave Andrews has stated, "to *quote* these Be-Attitudes is religious - but to *act* on them is revolutionary."[8] It is this reason - the fact that looking at these verses as more than mere platitudes requires action of us - that the Beatitudes are more often than not dismissed and ignored in the modern Church.

<u>The Beatitudes</u>

> "When Jesus saw the crowds, he went up
> the mountain; and after he sat down, his
> disciples came to him. Then he began to
> speak, and taught them, saying:
>
> 'Blessed are the poor in spirit, for theirs is
> the kingdom of heaven.

---

[8] Dave Andrews, *Plan Be* (Franklin: Authentic, 2008), 66.

'Blessed are those who mourn, for they will
be comforted.

'Blessed are the meek, for they will inherit
the earth.

'Blessed are those who hunger and thirst for
righteousness, for they will be filled.

'Blessed are the merciful, for they will
receive mercy.

'Blessed are the pure in heart, for they will
see God.

'Blessed are the peacemakers, for they will
be called children of God.

'Blessed are those who are persecuted for
righteousness' sake, for theirs is the
kingdom of heaven.

'Blessed are you when people revile you and
persecute you and utter all kinds of evil

against you falsely on my account. Rejoice

and be glad, for your reward is great in

heaven, for in the same way they persecuted

the prophets who were before you."[9]

Blessed are the poor in spirit, those who mourn, the meek, those who seek righteousness, who are merciful, who are pure in heart, who are peacemakers, and who are persecuted. It is no coincidence that Jesus begins his message with these remarks. These powerful first shots are aimed directly at revealing the stark difference between the society God dreams of and the society created through the violence of empire, a system gladly upheld by the religious authorities and ruling elite of Jesus' day. This is not Jesus merely "setting the stage" and laying down the platform of God's kingdom; this is Jesus delivering a very open and blunt rebuke of public and religious officials and all who benefited from their injustices.

To fully comprehend the situation that Jesus was addressing, we need to first look at the world during his time. Before the

---

Roman occupation of Jerusalem, the Jewish people surrounding Judea were mostly agricultural farmers, living off of what they planted and sowed. With Roman placement of the Herodian puppet lordship, this society drastically changed. The Jews who once farmed their land, the land of their family ancestors, were bought or forced out of their homes and became laborers and servants to the new owners of the land they used to call their own. No longer was the farming of the land simply for the means of feeding your family, but now was for mass production for the Herodian lordship, and in turn, the Roman Empire. Furthermore, the new owners of this land sought to use as little laborers as possible in order to reap higher profits, creating an even larger homeless and impoverished class. Many Jewish peasants became day-laborers, looking for work in carpentry or construction as they could. Though there were always the rich elite and those that were poverty-stricken, this new class structure created an even greater gap between the rich and poor, and it created an even greater number of those on the margins of Jewish society.

Yet Rome was not content to simply create a puppet lordship through Herod, and later, his sons. The Roman Empire also sought cooperation with the religious leaders of Jewish society. The temple priests were the central nervous system for most of Judaism and acted dually as both religious and political leaders. Rome knew this and therefore co-opted the Temple, turning the office of High Priest into a political appointment, tasked with keeping the order of Roman rule. Rather than observing the Jewish conscriptions on the office of High Priest and the length of term, Rome replaced them as they saw fit or as politically necessary. This further created an elite class within Judea. No longer were the appointments of temple priests reserved for the Levites, as commanded in Jewish scripture, but now any male from the elite class that had favor among Herod or Rome could be consecrated to this sacred office. The Temple instituted not only a monetary offering for the upkeep of the Temple and its priests, but also an annual Temple Tax that was given as tribute to Rome.

This is the world that Jesus entered. The reality of Jesus' world, where he grew up among the Jewish peasant class, should not be lost on us as we read through any of his teachings and how he understands what God desires in this world.

These opening declarations of what is acceptable and ethical in God's unkingdom are the first way in which Jesus sets up the unkingdom against the empire. Through these opening volleys, we see what Jesus was against was the system of domination that had turned the Temple of Jerusalem into a center and symbol of oppression, domination, and collaboration with the Roman Empire. Jesus stood opposed to the temple priests, the scribes, and the elders that used the God of Judaism and Torah to justify and to legitimize the Roman occupation, upper class elitism, massive taxation and tribute to a foreign ruler, and the creation of a peasant/serf class.

Blessed are the poor in spirit.

This is in stark contrast to many of the temple priests, scribes, and elders that used the Temple and God to justify such excesses at the expense of the poor and oppressed. These elite men saw themselves as "abundant in spirit" and "blessed." To dig further, the word "poor" used in this sentence is the Greek word *ptochos*, which means to literally "crouch or cower as one who is helpless." To the beggar, the ones living in abject poverty and the margins of

Roman/Jewish society, they were totally dependent upon others for help with even life's most basic necessities.

This cry from the poor can be heard not only from the echoes of empires past but also in the empires of today. In our American Empire, the poor also work for slave wages, often having to work multiple jobs simply to provide the most meager of necessities. The system, as in any empire, is set up to accumulate wealth for the political and elite class - always from the exploitation of the poor. This system creates a type of diseased symbiosis: with the powerful surviving and maintaining their opulence through the production and work of the poor, and the vulnerable masses relying on the very systems and powerful elite that have impoverished them to provide them with the bare essentials. As in Jesus' time, the American Empire sets its system up to view the wealthy and the elite as those who are blessed by God and in God's favor. It is the poor, by society's standards, who should be ashamed at their predicament - at their evident abandonment by God for being in such a lowly and embarrassing state.

Jesus flips the dominant social narrative with his first blessing. To claim that the poorest of the poor are truly blessed flies in the face of the status quo, which declares that blessings are counted by accumulated wealth and status. This statement of empowerment would not be lost on the migrant workers who were listening to Jesus' message. Nor was it lost on the religious and political elite who had amassed great wealth off the backs of the impoverished workers' labor.

Blessed are those who mourn.

Throughout the Jewish and Christian scriptures, the idea of mourning is synonymous with a deep anguish that is experienced when it is perceived that God has cast judgment upon someone, or appears to be distant and/or silent. Surely the Jewish working-class, which made up the majority of the Jewish population, would have understood and experienced the idea of mourning due to the notion that God had grown distant and silent with the Roman occupation's boot upon Jewish society's throat. I imagine that Jesus was not the only Jew during this time period to quote the Psalmist:

"My God, my God; why have you forsaken me? Why are you so far from helping me, from the words of my groaning?"[10]

With this declaration, that those who mourn are blessed in God's unkingdom, Jesus is sharing with his listeners that God is not distant, but has in fact drawn near. Jesus shares that God hears their cries amid the calamity and chaos of empire and considers them blessed and counted as great in God's unkingdom.

Blessed are the meek.

In the land of Roman Rule, the bold, the brave, the hotheaded, and the powerful are the ones who got what they wanted. They are blessed because they receive whatever they demand of others, regardless of whether "the other" can spare it or not. Jesus reverses this role by stating that those who are not in places of power, who are not reckless and who keep their anger in check, are the truly blessed. We can almost hear Jesus reword this statement as: "Blessed are those with self-restraint." Everyone gets angry, but those that count themselves as citizens of God's unkingdom do not allow that anger to become aggression and turn towards acts of

----

[10] Psalm 22:1

unchecked violence. Instead they allow their anger to motivate them to create justice in creative ways.

Blessed are those who desire righteousness.

Jesus' use of the words "hunger" and "thirst" evoke the images of those who have a driving need to satiate a desire in the very depths of their souls. Again, Jesus is not only referring to those who desire a personal righteousness. Here he is squarely pointing the finger at the religious elite that belonged to the Temple as well as the deep, unquenched desire of the Jewish people to see righteousness once again flow from the Temple and the lips of its leaders. Jesus declares that this deep hunger and thirst will be "filled" because the unkingdom of God is not only on its way, but has already arrived. God has drawn near and injustice cannot remain before God for long without dissolving.

Blessed are the merciful.

There are many things that the Roman Empire is famous for. Mercy is not one of them. Romans spoke of four cardinal virtues, which they adopted from the Greek philosophers Aristotle and Plato. These virtues were as follows:

Wisdom

Justice

Temperance

Courage

The idea of mercy as a virtue is nowhere to be found. In fact, it

was ingrained into every Roman citizen to despise pity and to see it

as a weakness.[11] Many of the Pharisees were harsh in their

judgments of others and showed a lack of mercy towards the ones

they claimed to serve. We see further in Matthew's Gospel that

Jesus rebukes them for this lack of mercy:

> "Wretched are you, you scribes and
>
> Pharisees. You hypocrites! For you tithe
>
> mint, dill, and cummin, and have ignored
>
> the more important matters of the law:
>
> justice and mercy and faith. It is these you
>
> should have practiced without neglecting the
>
> others."[12]

---

[11] John W. Ritenbaugh, *The Forerunner Commentary* (Bibletools.org, 1992) Mt. 5:5.

Do you see a similarity in our own culture? Mercy is also seen as a weakness. From the prisoner on death row begging for clemency to the idolization of a war hero that unflinchingly slaughtered America's foes, mercy is not in our vocabulary. Empire, be it Roman or American, does not apologize for its actions. Empire and those that are at its seats of power take what they want and care less for the repercussions.

Jesus calls this adherence to the whims of empire into question. How can we expect to call ourselves followers of a merciful God when we refuse to show mercy ourselves?

Blessed are the pure of heart.

I contend that this statement is not simply a goal Jesus set for those truly serious about following God and being a part of God's unkingdom. But it is also a direct jab at many of the religious elite who attempted to desperately gain this purity through the observances of thousands of rituals, laws, and rules to "the letter" without fulfilling and/or recognizing their "intent."

---

12 Matthew 23:23

Christianity, by and large, has become a religion of ritual. Go to church on Sunday. Accept Jesus as your "Personal Savior" and follow him. Leave church Sunday afternoon and return to your life unchanged. Rinse. Repeat.

Look deeper. It's been ingrained in us through both liberal and conservative mainstream Christian ideologies that we adhere to a specific set of values, never straying off the course. In conservative Christian circles, it is expected of you to unwaveringly support the Republican Party and take up the bold, yet hypocritical label of "pro-life". (This conservative anti-abortion stance is hypocritical due to its insistence that all life is sacred and should be nurtured, all the while supporting conservative policies that cut Welfare benefits to poor and impoverished families, advocating for the capital punishment, and supporting war.) This stance is mostly a knee-jerk, reactionary ritual that most conservative Christians feel that they must simply support, without question or thought, to be included into the Christian clique.

Likewise, more liberal-leaning mainstream Christianity - while it is thankfully much more inclusive and open than its counterpart -

still cannot fully let go of the grip it has on American nationalism and the politics of privilege. An association with the Democratic Party is a given, along with a belief in American capitalism, and patriotism. By merely adhering to ritual in order to "fit in", both conservative and liberal mainline churches have allowed themselves to be holy chaplains and apologists for a corrupt nation, making themselves gatekeepers for who is "in" and who is "out" of the circle of grace.

This adherence to religious ritual without letting the actual message of Jesus move us to change our hearts is the very notion that Jesus was speaking about. We've become a Christianity that has convinced itself that as long as we *believe* the "right things" and go through the "right" motions, we're doing what God wants us to do. Scripture, through the prophets, has revealed time and again that God doesn't want our ceremonies, worship, or rituals - God wants our hearts to open up and love; to seek to upend the systems of oppression and violence. The prophet Amos shares God's desire for more than empty words and practices when he wrote:

"I detest your religious festivals and your

gatherings; they reek of emptiness. You

bring me burnt offerings and grain

offerings, but I will not accept them. You

bring me your choice fellowship offerings,

but I don't care. Stop the clamor of your

songs. I will not listen to the music of your

instruments. Instead, let justice roll down

like a might river and righteousness like a

never-ending stream!"[13]

As Shane Claiborne penned in his book *The Irresistible Revolution,* "How can we worship a homeless man on Sunday and ignore one on Monday?"[14] Jesus' point was that when we attempt to follow God simply through ritual and rules, the heart remains unchanged. Jesus would go on to further illustrate this point with the parable of The Good Samaritan in Luke's Gospel.[15]

---

[13] Amos 5:21-24

[14] Shane Claiborne, *The Irresistible Revolution: Living As an Ordinary Radical* (Grand Rapids, MI: Zondervan, 2006), 18.

[15] Luke10:25-37

This lesson will come full-circle as Jesus continues with his sermon. One of the most central lessons of God's unkingdom is its commitment to seeking and practicing nonviolence. The Greek word used here for peace is *"eirene."* The definition of eirene is an absence of conflict, and also a reconciliation of both parties that results in a health, prosperity, and the well being of all.

Not only is Jesus calling his listeners to seek reconciliation as well as to reconcile, he is also pointing out a stark difference between God's unkingdom and earthly empire. Where empire would conquer and attain by force and violence, the unkingdom of God overcomes through love and compassion.

This message is two-fold. First, as pointed out above, you have the differences in how an empire such as Rome solves its problems and expands, versus the methods found in God's unkingdom and its citizens. The second part is the all too real understanding of the many violent uprisings from Jewish peasants against the Roman occupiers. These uprisings were quickly subdued and their leaders were made an example of through torture and graphic public executions.

Jesus is revealing that his fellow Jews have been attempting to overthrow the Master by using the master's tools and the sole tactic of violence has proven ineffective. Jesus proposes a different way, the way of the unkingdom, which uses active, nonviolent resistance and love to overcome oppressive forces. This is not to say that Jesus' conviction in nonviolence viewed the oppressed who saw violence as their only response as something evil or "wrong". To suggest that Jesus saw no difference between the revolutionaries that attempted to take down an oppressive regime and the actual oppressive regime is the highest form of victim shaming. Like the many fence-sitters in recent times who have declared that they are incapable of seeing the difference between anti-fascists and actual fascists who perpetrated the violence[16], this type of indifference towards violence is problematic at best, and ultimately has you siding with the oppressor.

---

[16] www.theguardian.com/world/2017/oct/08/neo-nazi-cowards-white-nationalists-charlottesville-rally

While I remain convinced that the gospels reveal that Jesus believed that nonviolence was not just a resistance tactic, but a philosophical way of life, I find the notion that Jesus would condemn the oppressed for using violence to fend off their oppressors as a ridiculous notion. Loving someone – even (especially) your enemy – is a rejection of our world's addiction to violence. However, sometimes you have to knock over the oppressing forces, (or a money-changer's table), that are actively and violently oppressing others to reveal love towards all parties. You cannot love the oppressed if you are not willing to stop the violence being perpetuated on them by the oppressor. As Mario Savio once said in his impassioned speech at the University of California in 1964, "…you've got to put your bodies upon the gears and upon the wheels, upon the levers, upon all the apparatus, and you've got to make it stop!"[17]

Blessed are those who are persecuted for righteousness' sake.

The Greek word *dioko*, which is translated as "persecute," literally means "to pursue, to follow after, to put to flight, or to

---

[17] Seth Rosenfeld, *Subversives: The FBI's War on Student Radicals, and Reagan's Rise to Power* (London: Macmillian, 2012), 216-217.

drive away." Within the context of the rest of the themes Jesus has presented in the Beatitudes, this persecution should be viewed in context with oppression, tyranny, and martyrdom. These three words were synonymous to the Jew living under Roman Rule.

One such story that would no doubt be fresh in the minds of Jesus' listeners was the election of Pontius Pilate to the position of Governor of Judea. According to the Jewish historian Flavius Josephus, one of Pilate's first orders of business was to erect statues of Caesar within the Temple grounds. As one can imagine, this edict did not go over well with the Jewish people and the men gathered within the Temple grounds to protest the placement of these idols.

> "On the ensuing day Pilate took his seat on
> his tribunal in the great stadium and
> summoning the multitude, with the apparent
> intention of answering them, gave the
> arranged signal to his armed soldiers to
> surround the Jews.

Finding themselves in a ring of troops, three deep, the Jews were struck dumb at this unexpected sight. Pilate, after threatening to cut them down, if they refused to admit Caesar's images, signaled to the soldiers to draw their swords.

Thereupon the Jews, as by concerted action, flung themselves in a body on the ground, extended their necks, and exclaimed that they were ready rather to die than to transgress the law. Overcome with astonishment at such intense religious zeal, Pilate gave orders for the immediate removal of the standards from Jerusalem."[18]

Jesus is telling his listeners to hold fast and to continue the pursuit of righteousness, even in the face of persecution; for the reign of Rome will not last forever, but the reign of God's justice is without end. Do not worry about what the temporary powers can

---

[18] Flavius Josephus, *Jewish Antiquities*, 18:55-59

do or threaten to do. Instead focus on the goodness that is in God whose reign is eternal and what you can do to make this possible.

<u>Salt and Light</u>

Following the Beatitudes, which revealed the qualities of a citizen in God's unkingdom, Jesus describes how we are to put these convictions into action:

> "You are the salt of the earth; but if salt has lost its taste, how can its saltiness be restored? It is no longer good for anything, but is thrown out and trampled under foot.
>
> You are the light of the world. A city built on a hill cannot be hidden. No one after lighting a lamp puts it under the bushel basket, but on the lampstand, and it gives light to all in the house. In the same way, let your light shine before others, so that they may see your good works and give glory to your Father in heaven."[19]

Jesus compares those who join in this new unkingdom, his disciples, with the salt of the earth and the light of the world.

Theologian John Howard Yoder explains "it is assumed that there should be something about the behavior of [Jesus'] disciples which will communicate to the world around."[20] Unitarian Minister Adin Ballou wrote that Jesus' comments of being the salt of the earth and the light of the world means not waiting "till the bad cease from aggression." It meant, rather, to be good, even if it means to suffer wrong rather than do wrong. We are called by our Teacher to overcome evil with good."[21] The idea that the disciples should be the medium by which the salt and the light, that is, the message of Jesus - the unkingdom of God - should be brought into the world and how this unkingdom was to overcome even the most powerful of empires.[22] As "salt and light," Jesus is calling his listeners to be the emissaries of God's unkingdom, by not only living in a way that is counter-cultural, but by speaking out against

---

[19] Matthew 5:13-16

[20] John Howard Yoder, *The Original Revolution* (Scottdale, PA: Herald Press, 1972), 41.

[21] Adin Ballou, *Christian Non-Resistance* (Philadelphia, PA: Universal Peace Union, 1910), 16.

[22] Baker alludes precisely to such witness in Baker, Christi-Anarchy, para. 13.

the status-quo, and revealing that another world is possible.

Christians should therefore speak out and not shy away from

denouncing the State when it behaves in an unchristian way -

especially in a nation such as the United States, where a majority of

the political leaders claim Christianity as their faith.

3
<u>THE TOPPLING OF THE HIERARCHY</u>

I remember a friend of mine complaining about a traffic citation he received on his way to work. Needless to say, he was less than happy about the incident. The way in which he recounted the event reveals a deep flaw within laws, legalism, and those that enforce it.

"Of course I was speeding," my friend said, "We all do it." He then goes on to describe how many traffic laws that the police officer broke in order to catch up to him and pull him over: "After spotting me with a radar, this cop made an illegal u-turn into traffic, weaving in and out of lanes in between cars at a high rate of speed — all to charge me with breaking one law."

Often times, the focus on a law distracts us from the actual intent. Even more often, the keepers and enforcers of the law point their fingers at those who ignore *unjust* rules while actually breaking *just* laws themselves.

Issues such as this were evident in Jesus' day, as well. This Rabbi's words were so radical, so challenging, and so thought-provoking, that many of his critics claimed he was undermining the whole of the Torah and all the Jewish Prophets that came before him. Jesus responds to this criticism by stating:

> "Do not think that I have come to abolish the law or the prophets; I have come not to abolish but to fulfill. For truly I tell you, until heaven and earth pass away, not one letter, not one stroke of a letter, will pass from the law until all is accomplished. Therefore, whoever breaks one of the least of these commandments and teaches others to do the same, will be called least in the kingdom of heaven; but whoever does them and teaches them will be called great in the kingdom of heaven. For I tell you, unless your righteousness exceeds that of the scribes and Pharisees, you will never enter the kingdom of heaven."[23]

This passage helps remind us of an often forgotten and integral piece of Jesus: he was a devout, practicing Jew. How do we look at this declaration by Jesus when Christianity, as far back as 100C.E.,[24] appears to be diametrically opposed to the ritual practices and many laws that were set forth through Torah/Mosaic Law? One of my heroes, author Leo Tolstoy, insisted that "The Old Law" is incompatible with Jesus' teachings and that it is "impossible to abide by both."[25] This leaves us with a difficulty.

Without going into debate regarding what Jesus might have actually said versus what the gospel-writers wrote to create a story that was compatible with Jesus' message and actions,[26] we are left with the obvious difficulty of reconciling what Jesus stated in Matthew's Gospel and the schism between Judaism and Christianity. In Matthew, it states that he came to fulfill the law and

---

[23] Matthew 5:17-20

[24] Even longer, if you would like to consider, as many scholars do, the destruction of the Temple in 77C.E. As the official split between Judaism and Christianity.

[25] Leo Tolstoy, *What I Believe*, (London: Elliot Stock, 1885), 64.

[26] I invite you to not only discover the resource of the theory regarding The Gospel of Q, but also the Jesus Seminar that has scholars and theologians from all stripes discuss this very topic.

not do away with it, yet many of his teachings and actions appear, at least on the surface, to contradict this declaration.[27]

I have to depart from Tolstoy in this instance and claim that Jesus' message and the true intent of the Torah, to love your neighbor and love God, are indeed compatible. I believe that Jesus did not see that his message was in conflict with the intent of Mosaic Law. Rather, I believe that Jesus saw that his message was in conflict with the way the religious elite were interpreting the Torah, and that it was being stifled by keeping "God in a box" and creating a hierarchy.

This declaration by Jesus regarding his adherence to the Torah again reveals, beyond a shadow of a doubt, that he was a devout Jew and saw himself as an observant follower of Mosaic Law. Through this lens, we see Jesus as being a part of a long line of prophets and teachers who continued to reinterpret, reinvent, and push the boundaries of what it means to follow Torah/Mosaic Law within a society fueled by God's grace. It is through this

---

[27] I get how the word "law" ruffles the feathers of fellow anarchists and radicals. I still abide by the Christian Anarchist, Ammon Hennacy's declaration to a judge while on trial for breaking a law: "Oh Judge, you and your damn laws. The righteous don't need them and the wicked ignore them. What good are they?"

understanding that we see the teachings and radical message of Jesus as being a continuation of the narrative from the Jewish Scriptures.

To gain a full perspective on how Jesus could claim he was not abolishing the Mosaic Law, while at the same time appearing to disregard or break portions of the Torah altogether, we must look at the gospel and historical context as a whole.

Jesus refers to two things further on in the gospel accounts - a "binding and loosing" of teachings and his disciples bearing his "yoke".[28] In Jesus' time, there were two main schools of Rabbinical Thought - The teachings of Rabbi Shammai and the teachings of Rabbi Hillel. Not just any rabbi could reinterpret the Torah, as Rabbis Shammai, Hillel, and Jesus himself did. In the Jewish tradition, only those who had "authority" could reinterpret Torah, and that authority could only be given by two other Teachers or Leaders that already held that authority.

This is why, in Matthew 7:29, it stated that Jesus "taught as one who had authority." At the beginning of the Gospel narrative Jesus

---

[28] Matthew 16:13-20 and 11:28-30, respectively.

was baptized by John the Baptizer, giving Jesus authority, and the Spirit of God came upon Jesus declaring its pleasure with him, giving Jesus his second vote of authority.[29] After so many generations passed from the original hearers of the gospel-accounts, it becomes difficult for us to fully understand all things within the scriptures without looking at the historical context. Without understanding the history of rabbinical teachings and schools of thought, we would go on thinking that passages that claimed Jesus "taught with authority" simply meant he was a good and powerful speaker. Furthermore, without an understanding of these real-life historical contexts, we would completely miss why it was so important for the gospel-writers to include Jesus being baptized by John the Baptizer and God's spirit coming down and commending Jesus' message.

All rabbis could teach from the Torah, the Prophets, and the Writings, but only through the interpretations that had been handed down from authority-bearing rabbis throughout the years. However, rabbis that held "authority" could reinterpret the

---

[29] Matthew 3:13-17.

scriptures (as we see Jesus doing with the Sermon on the Mount). When a rabbi that held authority was teaching Torah, he would either enforce a law as it was already interpreted, in effect "binding" it, or he would release his students from a law, also known as "loosening" - reinterpreting or rejecting altogether a law they deemed no longer applied. This collection of teachings a rabbi would bind or loosen would be called his "yoke".

This was no doubt a great point of contention between Jesus and the Religious Elite of his day. He taught as one who had authority, and then claimed that his authority came from not only God, but from John the Baptizer – a teacher whom a great deal of the Pharisees, Sadducees, and scribes abhorred. Not only did they consider Jesus' declaration that God had given him authority to preach and teach as blasphemy, but his other "authority" came from a man who they despised. This displeasure the religious elite had with John the Baptizer stemmed from his popularity with the Jewish people and his radical message of being reconciled with God through simple repentance, as well as his outright animosity towards the Pharisees and Sadducees, calling them a "brood of vipers" who refuse to repent while displaying religious piety.[30]

Within a historical context, we can see that Jesus and his hearers saw him as a teacher/rabbi/prophet who taught with authority. Therefore, according to Jewish tradition, Jesus was keeping the Torah completely intact, binding and loosening portions of the law and creating his own yoke. Through this viewpoint we can now see what, on the surface, appears to be deliberate violations of Torah by Jesus and his followers as actually a furthering of the Law and bringing it into a deeper understanding of love and justice. This is where Jesus' last jab comes into play - "For I tell you, unless your righteousness exceeds that of the scribes and Pharisees, you will never enter the kingdom of heaven." Jesus didn't think the Pharisees and scribes were righteous. He saw the religious elite going through the rituals, following the letter of the law but not actually living out the love and justice that Torah was created to produce.[31] When Jesus told his audience that they had to be more righteous than the religious elite he was essentially saying,

---

[30] Matthew 3:7-10.

[31] The Prophets before Jesus also faced this problem of legalism and attempted to correct it, with the prophets Samuel, Isaiah, Jeremiah, Amos, and Micah declaring that God was tired of all their festivals, rituals, and sacrifices - to abandon these things that had become merely fake acts of righteousness and, instead, practice justice, love, and mercy (1 Sam. 15:22, Is. 1:14, Jer. 7:21-23, Amos 5:21-24, Mic. 6:6-8).

"Don't just go through the motions of following the letter and forgetting the intent. Let Torah live within in you and create an outpouring of love and justice that only comes through God above."

The Synoptic Gospels give us back-to-back examples of Jesus not just reinterpreting Mosaic Law, but bringing out its fullness to the Pharisees in order to create "pushback" against their feigned-righteousness, revealing a God of love and justice. Jesus called them out on their false piety. From eating grain and healing on the Sabbath, to ignoring Jewish food restrictions and eating with publicans, sinners, and prostitutes. Jesus forgave a woman "caught in the act" of adultery and he touched lepers and menstruating women. He even created street theatre, going into the Temple and threw over the moneychanger's tables, scattering coins and running off sacrificial animals throughout the temple courts – the house of God! To the Jewish elite Jesus was a troublemaker. To the pious Pharisees and scribes he ignored and broke Torah. However, Jesus, like the prophets before him, was living out the core of Mosaic Law. He saw that if the interpretation of Torah got in the way of truly loving another person, then it must be reinterpreted or abandoned altogether.

This is why many of the Jewish religious elite were the focus of much of Jesus' scorn. If Jesus was not using them in his stories to play the role of the villain or foil, he was calling them out directly as hypocrites for following the letter of the law and missing its intent. He insisted that they sought the glory of men over the glory of God and ignored the matters of justice and compassion from the very Torah that they claimed to uphold. Jesus called them sons of the devil, proclaimed that they were whitewashed tombs, and that nothing out of their mouths produced life. Jesus claimed that their understanding of Torah and practices murdered the prophets.

Jesus not only fulfills Torah, as he claimed, but redefines it; drawing a metaphorical line in the sand by deliberately casting aside or reinterpreting that which no longer applies to those in a covenant of grace ("binding" and "loosening"). He reclaimed the spirit in which the Law was written, and which its "keepers" had corrupted.

4

<u>KILLING THE TOXIC CULTURE</u>

Continuing the topic of redefining Torah, Jesus delves further in overturning the traditional, hierarchal interpretations of Mosaic Law in society. Touching on almost all aspects of cultural structures – be it misogyny, pledging allegiance, or permissible State-sanctioned violence, there was no sacred cow Jesus was unwilling to tip over. Jesus begins with subject of anger and violence:

> "You have heard that it was said to those of ancient times, 'You shall not murder'; and 'whoever murders shall be liable to judgment.' But I say to you that if you are angry with a brother or sister, you will be liable to judgment; and if you insult a brother or sister, you will be liable to the council; and if you say, "You fool", you will be liable to the hell of fire. So when you are offering your gift at the altar, if you remember that your brother or sister has

something against you, leave your gift there
before the altar and go; first be reconciled to
your brother or sister, and then come and
offer your gift. Come to terms quickly with
your accuser while you are on the way to
court with him, or your accuser may hand
you over to the judge, and the judge to the
guard, and you will be thrown into prison.
Truly I tell you, you will never get out until
you have paid the last penny."[32]

One of the greatest points that is missed in Western Christianity, and in our cult worship of Nations and their military might, is this teaching of Jesus. On the surface, it appears that Jesus is simply asking us not to be angry, but this teaching delves so much deeper. This teaching, like all of Jesus' teachings, challenges our notions and preconceptions of what it means to follow God and to be counted as citizens in God's unkingdom. This declaration by Jesus should make us think twice about placing our faith in

---

[32] Matthew 5:21-37

temporal nations, much less placing those temporal nations' flags in our Churches - the unkingdom of God's "embassies".

"You have heard that it was said to those of ancient times, 'You shall not murder'; and 'whoever murders shall be liable to judgment.' But I say to you that if you are angry with a brother or sister, you will be liable to judgment..." To Jesus, the act of killing was not the only problem. Killing was the final outcome of the cancerous disposition that creates a judgmental attitude that allows the killing of others to take place.

In God's unkingdom, Jesus declares that evil is not simply in the act of murder - be it through the barrel of a soldier's gun, capital punishment, or a "run-in" with cops – but it is also the unchecked anger against another that is allowed to fester to the point of harming your sister or brother. This declaration by Jesus put the Roman Empire, and Jewish authorities in the crosshairs. Jesus implicates that the State goes against the unkingdom of God before it even commits the act of murder, be it through war, defamation, or capital punishment. According to Jesus, the State commits wrongdoing simply by passing judgment on another and then creating arguments/rationalizations for the accused's death.

It is in this understanding that Jesus is telling us to not be overcome by anger. Jesus does not actually command his hearers to never be angry. He is instead speaking about the vicious cycle of anger and violence that we find ourselves stuck in much too frequently. Jesus is calling us to keep our anger in check, and to show self-restraint and not be the aggressor, lest it fester and become cancerous, destroying others and ourselves in the process.

As I pointed out earlier, when Jesus blessed the meek in the Beatitudes, he is blessing those who are not filled with unchecked anger, nor filled with passivity and ambivalence. Jesus desires that we hold a righteous indignation against the wrongs and injustices in this world. To be sure, the Greek word that Jesus uses in the Beatitudes for "meek" is *praus*. This word does not mean "passive," as it is often misunderstood. Rather, meekness here means a controlled and channeled strength. This type of anger allows us to be upset at injustice and to stand up against oppression, be it through nonviolently taking punches on the Selma Bridge in the

United States Civil Rights Movement, or the overturning of tables and running the sacrificial animals out of the Temple during a Passover Festival. This is anger that's kept in check and channeled through beautiful actions of godly resistance.

"...if you insult a brother or sister, (call them 'Raca'), you will be liable to the council; and if you say, "You fool", you will be liable to the hell of fire." For Jesus, the issue here is not that we have insulted another, but that we have intentionally viewed our brother or sister as "less than." Leo Tolstoy describes the insult *Raca* as meaning "one not worthy of being called a human being."[33] Tolstoy argues that by calling someone less than human or a stupid fool, we create a separation between one another.[34]

In the unkingdom of God, Jesus sees peace and equality as being key among its citizens. This is Jesus' contention with unchecked anger. He knows that it leads to discrimination and hatred of those that are unlike us - the tools of empire. The State maintains its hierarchies, its classes, and its power through

---

[33] Leo Tolstoy, *What I Believe*, (London: Elliot Stock, 1885), 72.

[34] Leo Tolstoy, *What I Believe*, (London: Elliot Stock, 1885), 209.

propaganda that pits its citizens against one another and other nations, perpetuating discrimination, anger, and hatred. When this propaganda is successfully implanted in the citizens' psyche, it becomes easy for the State to create justifications for anger, torture, murder and war. We have a tragically perfect example before us as literal concentration camps in the U.S. were constructed, placing 2,342 immigrant children in after ripping them from their parents at the southern border. (Despite the public outcry against the Trump Administration and ICE, many children have yet to be reunited with their families.)[35]

"Don't fall for the empire's propaganda traps and don't be like the vengeful, prideful empire," declares Jesus. "Don't allow perceived wrongdoing or your differences between one another to allow your anger to justify your violent desire to strike first. You're better than this; you were created for something so much greater." When we truly allow ourselves to see one another as children of God, anger to the point of violence and death will be impossible.

---

[35] www.usatoday.com/story/news/politics/2018/06/18/immigration-children-detention-center-cry-separated-parents/712292002/

Jesus continues, "So when you are offering your gift at the altar, if you remember that your brother or sister has something against you, leave your gift there before the altar and go; first be reconciled to your brother or sister, and then come and offer your gift. Come to terms quickly with your accuser while you are on the way to court with him, or your accuser may hand you over to the judge, and the judge to the guard, and you will be thrown into prison. Truly I tell you, you will never get out until you have paid the last penny."

"What is more important," Jesus asks us, "a sacrifice to God or reconciling ourselves with our sisters and brothers?" Jesus tells us to set the offering aside and seek forgiveness. In the unkingdom of God, forgiveness and reconciliation are the currencies of justice. The prophets from the Jewish Scriptures echo this teaching of reconciliation, of justice and righteousness, before any sacrifice, festival, or show of worship:

> "I hate, I despise your festivals, and I take
>
> no delight in your solemn assemblies. Even
>
> though you offer me your burnt-offerings

and grain offerings, I will not accept them;
and the offerings of well-being of your
fatted animals I will not look upon. Take
away from the the noise of your songs; I will
not listen to the melody of your harps. But
let justice roll down like waters, and
righteousness like an ever-flowing stream."[36]

"With what shall I come before the Lord,
and bow myself before God on high? Shall I
come before him with burnt-offerings, with
calves a year old? Will the Lord be pleased
with thousands of rams, with tens of
thousand of rivers of oil? Shall I give my
firstborn for my transgression, the fruit of
my body for the sin of my soul?' He has told
you, O mortal, what is good; and what does
the Lord require of you but to do justice, to

---

[36] Amos 5:21-24

love kindness, and to walk humbly with your

God?"[37]

"For I desire steadfast love and not sacrifice,

the knowledge of God rather than burnt-

offerings."[38]

The recurring theme of this section of his sermon is that Jesus is not commanding us to refrain from anger, but to seek reconciliation and justice above all things. Anger, for Jesus, was legitimate if it was used constructively and positively without returning evil for evil. Jesus teaches that unchecked anger is the catalyst for the vicious cycles of hatred and violence we continually find ourselves in. Jesus points to reconciliation with one another as the only cure. Augustine of Hippo, the early Christian writer, understood these passages concerning anger and wrote, "Hope has two beautiful daughters; their names are Anger and Courage. Anger at the way things are, and Courage to see that they do not remain as they are."[39]

---

[37] Micah 6:6-8

[38] Hosea 6:6

[39] Robert McAfee Brown, *Spirituality and Liberation: Overcoming the Great Fallacy*

"You have heard that it was said, 'You shall not commit adultery.' But I say to you that everyone who looks at a woman with lust has already committed adultery with her in his heart. If your right eye causes you to sin, tear it out and throw it away; it is better for you to lose one of your members than for your whole body to be thrown into Gehenna. And if your right hand causes you to sin, cut it off and throw it away; it is better for you to lose one of your members than for your whole body to go into Gehenna. 'It was also said, 'Whoever divorces his wife, let him give her a certificate of divorce.' But I say to you that anyone who divorces his wife, except on the ground of unchastity, causes her to commit

---

(Westminster: John Knox Press, 1988), 136.

adultery; and whoever marries a divorced woman commits adultery."[40]

Though Jesus is speaking specifically on marriage, divorce, and adultery, he continues his over-arching narrative - that it matters how we treat one another. Jesus is calling us to dig deeper and to get to the *root* of the convictions we have.

Everyone with a sense of morality knows that adultery is wrong. It is one of the deepest betrayals that can be perpetrated against the one(s) you have committed yourself to. Jesus is telling his audience that adultery does not start when sexual intercourse outside of the committed relationship begins - it starts in the heart. The desires and passion that we should have exclusively towards our partner are now shared with another who is outside of that committed relationship. Jesus is stating that if we refrain from planting these adulterous seeds, it will not come to bear fruit.

While adultery and the matters of the heart are the first issues addressed, Jesus is telling his audience that they must look at their world and those in it as more than mere sexual objects. Misogyny

---

[40] Matthew 5:27-32

and inequality are created when we men view women as objects created by God for our pleasure. Though much throughout the history of the Church has been created to perpetuate the inequality and subservience of the female sex, Jesus himself saw men and women as equals.

We see this with his election of the first evangelist: the woman at the well (Jn. 4:1-30), his accumulation of both male and female disciples (Lk. 8:1-3), and, according to the resurrection story, his choosing of Mary Magdalene to be "the apostle to the apostles," proclaiming that Jesus had arisen (Mt. 28:9, Mk. 16:9, Jn. 20:16). The early Church followed in this same ethic, which is evidenced by Paul's writings of Junia, whom he calls "an apostle among the apostle" in his letter to the Roman church (16:7) as well as in non-canonical texts, such as the *Sophia of Jesus Christ, Pistis Sophia, The Gospels of Thomas* and *of Mary Magdalene*, and the *1ˢᵗ Apocalypse of James.*[41] In Jesus' mind, to view one another as nothing more than

---

[41] *The Sophia of Jesus Christ* opens with "..his twelve disciples and the seven women continued to be his followers" traveling together. In the *Pistis Sophia*, Jesus calls upon his mother, Mary, Mary Magdalene, Salome, and Martha to witness to the mysteries of "The Greater Soul". *The Gospel of Thomas* reveals that Jesus valued Mary Magdalene as a great disciple – much to the chagrin of some of the other disciples. *The Gospel of Mary Magdalene* declares Mary, not Peter, as the one Jesus

sex objects is to devalue the indwelling of God within them. This is

further evidenced by Jesus' teaching on divorce.

When Jesus declares that "anyone who divorces his wife,

except on the ground of unchastity, causes her to commit adultery;

and whoever marries a divorced woman commits adultery" he is

speaking directly to males in his audience.

Like all patriarchal societies, the Jewish faith/ritual practices

had moved from a place where women like the prophet Miriam

(Ex. 15:20), the great Judge Deborah (Jg. 4:5; 5:7), the faithfulness

of Ruth, and the boldness of Queen Esther could be celebrated[42] to

a male dominated society, where women were mostly subjugated

and put to the letter of an extreme interpretation of Levitical Law,

being treated as chattel. This denigrating view of women colored

every aspect of Jewish life – including marriage and divorce.

---

entrusted to build his church upon. Finally, the *1ˢᵗ Apocalypse of James* states: "Yet another thing I ask of you: who are the seven women who have been your disciples? And behold all women bless you." Then reveals four of these women's names: "When you speak these words of this perception, encourage these four: Salome and Mariam and Martha and Arsinoe."

[42] So much so that the last two women mentioned had entire Biblical books named after them.

According to Jewish customs, a male could divorce his wife for anything – even the most trivial of grievances. As was the custom, when the husband divorced his wife, he could continue life as normal. However, the woman was given few options, as she had no property of her own and she was the caretaker of any children her and her spouse had. The only choices a divorced woman had were to either live on the street as a beggar with her children, become a prostitute, or remarry. The latter two, according to Jewish conventions of that time, condemned a woman as a whore and an adulteress.

Jesus obviously viewed this is as a major injustice. Therefore, his declaration against divorce and remarriage is not so much a sweeping judgment that encompasses all who divorce and remarry, such as those who leave an abusive spouse, or who divorce because their spouse abuses their children, etc., (as it is oft-interpreted, with disastrous results, in many churches today). This is a bold condemnation of the societal practices that allowed the male to divorce without repercussion, while the woman continually paid the price.

We can almost hear Jesus saying, "So if a woman is divorced and remarries, she commits adultery? Do you truly wish to play that game? Because when you divorce her for nothing, you are the cause of her being labeled a 'whore'. So if we're willing to call a divorced woman a whore and an adulteress, whoever remarries a divorced woman is a whore and adulterer, too. Let us stop labeling and devaluing one another with such ugliness. This type of behavior does not work in the unkingdom of God. Stop seeing yourself as better than others and start viewing one another as fellow children of God."

<u>Concerning Oaths</u>

Jesus moves from the personal and individual matters of the heart, which can manifest themselves into the public sphere, back to the power that dominates the public sphere, AKA the State.

> "Again, you have heard that it was said to
> those of ancient times, 'You shall not swear
> falsely, but carry out the vows you have
> made to the Lord.' But I say to you, Do not
> swear at all, either by heaven, for it is the

throne of God, or by the earth, for it is his

footstool, or by Jerusalem, for it is the city

of the great king. And do not swear by your

head, for you cannot make one hair white or

black. Let your word be "Yes, Yes" or "No,

No"; anything more than this comes from

evil."[43]

These verses are normally passed off and turned into cute little adages, like "Don't make promises you cannot keep". However, I think Jesus' intention with this admonition is much more radical. Jesus' issue with swearing oaths, or pledging allegiance to something other than the unkingdom of God is two-fold.

In a society such as ours, where we are pushed and coerced into reciting the United States' Pledge of Allegiance in our very first year of public childhood education, it is difficult to comprehend a God who calls upon us to refrain from attempting to serve both God's unkingdom and the earthly nation we reside in. Jesus is continually pushing his audience into the realization that in order to

---

[43] Matthew 5:33-37

embrace fully the unkingdom of God and accept love as the highest order, they have to reject those that have claimed lordship and authority for themselves, as well as the "tools" that were used in order to gain that power.

Like the Roman Empire of Jesus' day, our nation, was built and expanded upon through the unapologetic extermination and segregation of the indigenous people, through countless wars and skirmishes, and upon the backs of slave labor. As we face this stark and blunt reality, Jesus asks: "How is this worthy of your oath or your allegiance? How does this emperor and empire even come close to deserving the loyalty we are called to give God and God's unkingdom?" Jesus sees this act of fealty, this pledging of an oath - of allegiance - towards a corrupt and temporal regime, as so reprehensible that he declares we should leave God and all God has created out of it: "Do not swear at all, either by heaven, for it is the throne of God, or by the earth, for it is his footstool..." because God and God's liberating love cannot be found in empire.

Author R.V. Sampson, while expounding upon Leo Tolstoy's understanding of Jesus' prohibition of oath-taking, wrote, "Oath taking is fundamental to military and therefore political power. The oath of allegiance creates the legal basis for the maintenance of the disciplined unity of large numbers of men, on which all State power ultimately rests."[44] By Jesus calling upon his hearers to abstain from taking oaths, they are denying the State its assumed power; striking a challenging blow to the legitimacy of Caesar's reign and his regime.

It is no coincidence that, after his death, the earliest of Jesus' followers began calling Jesus "Lord", "King of Kings", "Son of God", and "Prince of Peace." These titles were ones they had usurped from Caesar, declaring that the unkingdom they are citizens of and the king they serve has turned the order of the world upside down (or, perhaps, right side up). To this small group, God had taken a poor peasant from a backwater town called Nazareth and placed him as "king."[45] It's an act of insurgency, rebellion, and

---

[44] R.V. Sampson, *Tolstoy: The Discovery of Peace* (London: Heinemann Educational Publishers, 1973), 172

[45] I use the term "king" loosely, as I believe Jesus' earliest followers did. We would be remiss if we overlooked the fact that Jesus was not interested in creating another monarchy, but in creating equality for all people, where no one had coercive power over another - even the gospels portray him literally running away when some of his hearers attempted to crown him their king (Jn. 6:15). Jesus' earliest followers used the term "king" when referring to Jesus or God in a two-fold sense: lampooning and rejecting what they viewed as the illegitimate

resistance. This band of dissidents placed their allegiance in the unkingdom of God and God as their "king," openly admitting treason to the earthly empire of Rome by rejecting any oath or act of allegiance that the Roman authorities demanded of them. This rebellion that the teachings and example of Jesus incited was one that revealed that a better way is possible through rejecting the powers and principalities, calling those in the places of power to repent and then join them in this new way of life.

Concerning Retaliation

Now, we move into one of the most difficult portions of Jesus' message - his teachings on how his followers were to react towards violence, oppression, and abuse.

> "You have heard that it was said, "An eye
>
> for an eye and a tooth for a tooth." But I say
>
> to you, Do not resist an evildoer. But if
>
> anyone strikes you on the right cheek, turn
>
> the other also; and if anyone wants to sue
>
> you and take your coat, give your cloak as

kingship of Caesar and declaring that Jesus' way and God are what lead them.

well; and if anyone forces you to go one mile, go also the second mile. Give to everyone who begs from you, and do not refuse anyone who wants to borrow from you."[46]

For millennia, we have attempted to rationalize or dismiss these teachings altogether. When we attempt to whitewash Jesus' message, we miss the fact that these illustrations of turning the other cheek, giving up your cloak, and going the extra mile are all based in a historical reality that created subversive political responses.

First, Jesus reveals that the long-held conviction of equal retaliation for a wrong, regardless of how justified this action may seem, is not the way of God's ukingdom.

"You have heard that it was said, 'An eye for an eye and a tooth for a tooth.' But I say to you, Do not resist an evildoer."

---

[46] Matthew 5:38-45

First, what does Jesus mean when he commands his hearers to not resist an evildoer? As author Walter Wink puts it: "The traditional interpretation of 'do not resist an evildoer' has been nonresistance to evil - an odd conclusion, given the fact that on every occasion Jesus himself resisted evil with every fiber of his being."[47] I think the answer is simple: when someone is committing an act of violence towards you, as a citizen of God's ukingdom, you are to get creative and attempt to find ways to not respond in kind. Here Jesus solidifies his declaration at the beginning of his sermon when he declared those that are peacemakers are blessed and counted as children of God.

For Jesus resistance was refusing to let your oppressor dictate the terms of the engagement; refusing to allow your only options be flight or fight. Jesus is calling upon his hearers to seek options other than violence and passivity. Walter Wink, again, calls this "third way" as something "that is at once assertive and yet nonviolent."[48]

---

[47] Walter Wink, *The Powers that Be: Theology for a New Millennium*, (New York, New York: Doubleday Press, 1998), 98.

[48] Walter Wink, *The Powers that Be: Theology for a New Millennium*, (New York, New York: Doubleday Press, 1998), 98.

Jesus gives us three examples for using nonviolence as a tactic, beginning with the most direct and immediate action of one who has assaulted you.

> "You have heard that it was said, 'An eye for an eye and a tooth for a tooth.' But I say to you, Do not resist an evildoer. But if anyone strikes you on the right cheek, turn the other also..."

During Jesus' time in ancient Rome, left-handed people were considered unlucky and untrustworthy. The word "sinister" actually derives from the Latin word for *left*. The right hand, which is the dominant hand for the majority of the population, was used for eating and social gestures. In turn, the left hand was used for cleaning yourself after you emptied your bladder or bowels. These societal conscriptions and designated tasks for the right hand and the left hand were imposed on all in the Roman Empire, regardless of what side might be your dominant. These practices helped create the ideas of the left hand being the "unclean" hand and the right hand being the "socially acceptable" hand.[49]

When Jesus speaks of someone hitting you on the right cheek, they would more than likely be using their right hand. The only way they could logically strike you on your right cheek, would be to use the back of their hand. To be struck with the back of someone's hand, or *back-handed*, was to be treated as a "lesser." To the person doing the striking, they are attempting to show that they are your "better," superior to you in every way. Our terminology for back-handing someone in the modern world, a "bitch slap" or a "pimp slap," reveals that the connotation of this type of strike is still meant to be derogatory and to treat someone as a "lesser."

How does Jesus teach his hearers to respond to such an insult? Jesus, in his continually brilliant fashion, rejects the two obvious responses of violent retaliation or submission, then reveals a third way:

Jesus tells his audience to turn the other cheek.

In doing this, Jesus reveals how to respond without striking back in violence. Jesus shares how to disarm our attacker by

---

[49] Stanley Coren, *Left-Handedness: Behavioral Implications and Anomalies* (Amsterdam: Elsevier Science Publishers B.V., 1990)

disarming ourselves. By refusing to retaliate with violence, the "superior being" that struck you has now been stripped of his/her power. Now if your attacker desires to continue their assault, he or she will be forced to slap you with their open palm, no longer using the "back-hand," as one would an inferior. You're forcing to strike you as an equal. Your refusal to move or retaliate in kind will either cause your assailant to desist in their attack, or if they desire to strike you again, it will reveal their brutality towards all that surround you.

It is as Mahatma Gandhi was to have stated about this lesson:

> "[I] suspected that Jesus meant one must show courage and be willing to take one blow or several blows to show that you will not strike back nor turn aside. That calls on something in the enemy that makes his hatred for you decrease and his respect for you increase."[50]

---

[50] Producer & Director Richard Attenborough. (1982). Gandhi. United Kingdom: Columbia Pictures.

This command wasn't supposed to be interpreted as promotion of passivity, or to "simply take the beating and do nothing about it." Jesus tells his hearers to stand up and resist! Defy the oppressors and refuse to be seen as a "lesser." Refuse to submit, yes, but play by a new "rule book," the way of God's unkingdom, which calls for us to respond in creative ways that is neither a violent response or a submissive resignation.

Jesus continues with his second example: "if anyone wants to sue you and take your coat, give your cloak as well."

In Jesus' time, your cloak was unlike a modern coat. This was not a garment you could simply take off when you became too hot, and then you still had a shirt and pants on underneath. No. When Jesus tells his audience to hand over their cloak to their accuser, he is telling them to strip naked.

But what's the point of stripping? What greater purpose does this serve? Doesn't openly displaying your naked body go against everything that Judaism stands for?

Despite Christianity's attempt to reinterpret all of the Jewish Scriptures within the context of their own theology, Judaism does not share the Christian view that nudity is sinful and exclusively sexual in nature. To the Jewish people public nudity was more concerned with shame. The Jewish people saw public nudity as an activity of war captives, like slaves being reduced to nothing, not even clothing. To the Jew, nudity in the Talmudic Period and beyond was seen as a barrier to regular Jewish practice, such as the recitation of the shema and daily prayers.

We see this thought process being with Adam and Eve's realization that they are naked in the story of the Garden of Eden. After they discover this fact they feel ashamed and cover their genitals with fig leaves.[51] Skipping a few chapters to the story of Noah, we find that Noah becomes intoxicated and passes out naked. His son, Ham, discovers him. Instead of covering his "shame," Ham runs to tell his siblings. Ham's brothers do what is virtuous and cover their father up. When Noah awakens and discovers what Ham did, he curses Ham's son, Canaan.[52]

---

[51] Genesis 3:74

[52] Genesis 9:20-27

This "shamefulness" of public nudity is also evident in the contempt the Maccabaees shared for the ancient Greek gymnasia - where the Greek men and boys would exercise either completely nude or in a loincloth. Reading further accounts in the 3rd - 4th CE writings in the *Sifre on Deuteronomy,* we find the writer interprets the "nation of fools" described in Deuteronomy 32:21 as being "those who come from Barbary and Mauretania and walk about naked in the marketplace." This conviction lines up perfectly with the Talmud, "for there is nothing more objectionable and abominable to the Omnipresent than the man who goes about naked in the streets."[53]

As we can see, public nudity is considered a shameful act within the Jewish culture of that time. When Jesus tells his audience to strip naked before his accusers and hand over his cloak, he is openly calling for public shame. However, in this act the offensiveness (or shame) would not be upon the one who became nude publicly. They would blame the one who demanded the cloak from the victim.

---

[53] Yebamoth 63b

Author Walter Wink explains how this act of public nudity that Jesus suggests would create a "stunning protest" against the powers that created violent injustice, which rendered a man naked.[54] To Jesus this is an example to reveal the "shame" of an entire system that creates large and oppressed working classes who are subservient and indebted at birth to the elite minority. It also affords the debt collector, and those who stand on the side of the elite, an opportunity to see just what these systemic practices bring upon the oppressed and to abandon their status. Jesus saw this example as an opportunity not just to shame, but for repentance.

Jesus moves into his last illustration: "and if anyone forces you to go one mile, go also the second mile."

In this analogy Jesus is making a direct reference to an established Roman military practice. This practice would allow a soldier to force a civilian into subservience and carry his equipment - but only for one mile (it was an infraction against the military code of conduct to have a civilian to walk more than a mile). This practice had real world implications and consequences. It did not

---

[54] Walter Wink, *Jesus' Third Way* (Random House Publications: New York, 1998), 103.

matter where you were or what you were doing, if a Roman Soldier came to you and demanded you carry his pack, you were obligated to do so. Imagine a day laborer (like many of Jesus' hearers were) in the middle of a job when a Roman Soldier came calling.

To its original hearers - before Jesus' instruction to "go an extra mile" became reduced to simply "do your best" - this meant something revolutionary. With Jesus' example, it allowed his hearers the opportunity to turn the status quo on its head.

Just imagine the scenario: A Roman Soldier tosses his pack at you, demanding you carry it for him. You must oblige, lest you be arrested, beaten, and/or killed. You begin walking with the Roman Soldier, the embodiment of the ones who stole your land and now occupy it - the *enemy*. You then reach your required mile destination and the Soldier orders you to hand his equipment back to him. Here is where he expects the typical response of obedience in handing the equipment over and the slave walking away in anger and disgust. What the soldier receives is something entirely different.

Instead of acting in the role the oppressor expects, Jesus tells his audience to respond differently. The oppressor instead replies, "No, we can go another mile. I'm good." The tables have now turned. Power has now shifted without the oppressed raising a hand in anger or violence. The one forced to carry the equipment is now in control, with the Roman Soldier, fully aware of the violation in having a civilian carry equipment for more than one mile, begging, threatening, and demanding for his trade tools to be returned.

With all three of these illustrations, which were all common practices those in power would employ upon the disenfranchised, Jesus offers responses that turn the societal structures on their ears. These three examples deny the oppressor of their supposed power, subvert their authority, and challenge the status quo by refusing to respond to the demands in the anticipated manner. This practice of active nonviolence empowers the victim and arms them with tools that tip the scales while throwing the oppressor off balance.

Again, I feel that I must emphasize that Jesus making the moral and just argument for nonviolence does not mean he is placing a moral judgement on those who have used or advocated for violence against oppressors. Jesus, being born into oppression, would be all-too-aware of the violence that many in his time were born into because of the injustice inherent in the system. An empire that continues to place generations of people into poverty and invest wholesale into a culture of violence and conquest has no other outcome but to give birth to violent opposition. How can Jesus, or we as Jesus's followers, judge anyone brought up in this type of system – be it from Roman times to the present – for responding back with violence? It is truly as Rev. Dr. Martin Luther King, Jr. stated: that a riot is the language of the unheard.

Jesus' conviction in nonviolence was not a statement that violence towards the oppressors is always ineffective, but that it is limited in its scope. To Jesus, violence has the ability to achieve strategic victories, but it can never create relationships or reconciliation. And this is at the heart of Jesus' message: if we've overthrown the oppressors and yet have no way towards reconciliation, then our children will fight their children as nothing was truly resolved.

It is this understanding of Jesus' message that causes the Christian Anarchist to be inherently nonviolent. Liberation theology and nonviolent direct action are essential principles that Christian Anarchism espouses for daily life. Actively resisting empire and other oppressive forces, rejecting greed and other capitalistic endeavors, seeking reconciliation, and caring for others, (despite these attributes being seen as "radical" by a "Christian Nation"), are central to the Christian faith. With this desire to act as citizens of God's unkingdom, displaying these peaceable and compassionate qualities, I'm afraid that here in West, we are collectively entering a "Bonhoeffer Moment".

Dietrich Bonhoeffer was a German theologian and minister, who saw the rise of the Third Reich for what it was: hatred, fear, misogyny, xenophobia, and racism masquerading as social good and justice. Bonhoeffer recognized this threat quickly and began to actively warn against the dangers of Nazism and its leader who attempted to make themselves an idol. Bonhoeffer even made a radio address calling out these warnings two days after Hitler took office.

Despite Bonhoeffer's commitment to nonviolence and loving one's enemies through his understanding of Jesus' message, he became a member of a coup attempt against Hitler and his fascist regime. Rev. Bonhoeffer wrote of this apparent contradiction, stating that he lived in a time where evil appeared as a "form of light, good deeds, historical necessity, social justice"[55] and argued that "as much as the Christian would like to remain distant from political struggle, nonetheless, even here the commandment to love urges the Christian to stand up for his neighbor."[56] Rev. Bonhoeffer saw Christian Churches throughout Germany filled with SS soldiers, Concentration Camp guards and doctors, and Nazi officers on Sunday mornings. The overall lack of rejection of Nazism by the Christian Church, and in many ways collusion, caused Bonhoeffer to see German Christianity as a willing participant in the evils of the regime – the German Church had become a chaplain of the Nazi Party. To Rev. Bonhoeffer, Christianity bore responsibility in the rise and acceptance of Hitler's fascist regime. And as a Christian, Bonhoeffer saw it as his responsibility to correct this error.

---

[55] Dietrich Bonhoeffer, *Letters and Papers from Prison,* (Fortress Press: Minnesota, 2010), 38.

[56] Dietrich Bonheoeffer, *Ecumenical, Academic, and Pastoral Work, 1931-1932,* (Fortress Press: Minnesota), 4.

Rev. Bonhoeffer was one of the first voices in Germany to rebuke the hatred of the Nazis publicly. Twelve years later he was executed by them as a traitor. May he rest in power.

Bonhoeffer's actions cause us as Christians to ask what we should do in the face of literal, physical violence being perpetrated against our sisters and brothers? Do we try to use peaceable means to engage and stop the attacks? Of course. But, as we've witnessed in multiple recent Neo-Nazi rallies, a call to conscience and love does not interest them.[57]

As Christians who identify as anarchist, I feel that we have to begin to find our footing somewhere in between Dorothy Day and Huey P. Newton. Violence should never be our first, second, third, etc., defense. But as Rev. Bonhoeffer also recognized, allowing the powers and principalities to actively dash our oppressed sisters and brothers into pieces while we are capable of possibly stopping them is the greater sin.

I invite you to wrestle with me in this.

---

[57] https://www.adl.org/news/press-releases/adl-report-white-supremacist-murders-more-than-doubled-in-2017

5

<u>CHANGING THE WAY WE RESIST</u>

The late anarchist folk singer, Utah Phillips, once described a conversation he had with his friend and mentor, Ammon Hennacy. Hennacy, a Christian Anarchist and an early member of the Catholic Worker Movement, told Phillips that, "You came into this world armed to the teeth with an arsenal of weapons. Weapons of privilege, economic privilege, sexual privilege, racial privilege. You want to be a pacifist? You're not just going to have to give up guns, knives, clubs, and hard, angry words. You are going to have to lay down the weapons of privilege and go into the world completely disarmed."[58]

Jesus immediately follows his examples on nonviolent resistance with a declaration for his hearers to love their enemies.

> "You have heard that it was said, 'You shall
>
> love your neighbor and hate your enemy.'
>
> But I say to you, Love your enemies and

---

[58] Ani DiFranco and Utah Phillips, *The Past Didn't Go Anywhere*, (Righteous Babe Records, 1996), Track Anarchy.

pray for those who persecute you, so that

you may be children of your Father in

heaven; for he makes his sun rise on the evil

and on the good, and sends rain on the

righteous and the unrighteous. For if you

love those who love you, what reward do

you have? Do not even the tax-collectors do

the same? And if you greet only your

brothers and sisters, what more are you

doing than others? Do not even the Gentiles

do the same? Be perfect, therefore, as your

heavenly Father is perfect."[59]

Jesus' instruction, like so many of his teachings, permeates

both the public and the political sphere, while also influencing the

personal ways we forgive and treat those we deem our "enemies".

In this teaching, Jesus challenges his hearers to reject the trappings

of nationalism and war, and he reveals that the act of loving one's

---

[59] Matthew 5:43-48

enemies - praying for and actively forgiving them - is the measure by which one will be known as a child of God.

The word "neighbor" used in this passage, as well as many other passages throughout our modern translations of scripture, is actually a mistranslation of the Hebrew word *reyacha*. Instead of this word meaning "a fellow inhabitant of this land," which is how we have been taught, *reyacha* actually means "fellow Jew."

Looking at this passage with *renewed* eyes, we see Jesus saying:

> *"You have heard that it was said, 'You shall love*
> *your fellow Jew and hate your enemy.' But I say to*
> *you, Love your enemies and pray for those who*
> *persecute you, so that you may be children of your*
> *Father in heaven;"*

The implications of reclaiming the understanding of this text are far-reaching.

Again we see Jesus' teachings lining up with the teachings of the great Prophets. The Prophets rejected the early notions of the people who would become the nation of Israel that held the notion that God not only condoned the invasion of Canaan, but commanded them to slaughter "every man, woman, and child" (1 Sam. 15:3) in the towns and city-states they desired to claim for their own.

The prophet Amos, who was the first of the great "Writing Prophets," wrote "Let justice roll down like the waters, and righteousness like an ever-flowing stream" (5:24). This passage reveals that the following of God and social justice, also known as loving others, are inseparable actions.

The prophet Micah continues this theme, asking the question: "And what does the Lord require of you?" He then answers it, "To act justly and to love mercy and to walk humbly with your God" (6:8).

The prophet Isaiah declared that God "shall judge between the nations, and shall arbitrate for may peoples; they shall beat their swords into plowshares, and their spears into pruning-hooks; nation shall not lift up sword against nation, neither shall they learn war anymore" (2:4).

Then we have Jesus, who follows suit by declaring that we should not simply resist in rising up against our enemies in violence, but that we are to actively love, care for, and pray for them.

The great author Leo Tolstoy sums up this passage in his book, *What I Believe*:

> "...the word 'enemy' is seldom used in the Gospels in a private or personal sense, but almost always in a public and national one..."

> "All the passages, spread over the different books of Scripture, in which it is prescribed to the Jews to oppress, slay, and destroy other nations, are brought together by Jesus into one saying, 'Thou shalt hate or do evil to thine enemy.' He says, 'You have been told to love your own people, and to hate the enemy of your race, but I tell you to love all without distinction of nationality.'"[60]

Tolstoy again cites this passage in *The Gospel in Brief* as he rewords it for his modern audience:

> "Love not only your own countrymen, but people of other nations also. Let others hate you, attack you, and wrong you, but speak well of them and do good to them. If you are attached only to your own countrymen, remember that all men are attached to their own countrymen, and wars result from that. But behave equally well to men of all nations, and you will be sons of the Father. All men are His children, so they are all brothers to you."[61]

Our modern governments and empires are not that different from those that original hearers of Jesus' message had to endure. "Love our enemies?" Our governments and empires ask. "People have to pay for their crimes and their offenses."

---

[60] Leo Tolstoy, *What I Believe* (Elliot Stock: London, 1885) p. 91

[61] Leo Tolstoy, *The Gospel in Brief* (Danish Peace Academy, 2007) p. 24

Most people agree with this line of thinking, including many Jews under Roman Rule in Jesus' day (and many Christians in our current time). The problem is that if we look at these passages correctly, we will see that empire's idea of justice is incongruent with Jesus' idea of justice. To the worldly systems of government, "justice" and "love" are separate entities. Jesus teaches us that God's justice cannot be enacted without love. In the unkingdom of God, love and justice cannot exist without one another.

This type of loving justice condemns the wrongdoing, but does not condemn the wrongdoer to some form of harsh punishment or ill-treatment. This love of enemies, while combating the wrong doings, also prays for them and works to convict the hearts - as the Apostle Peter did in his Pentecost Sermon (Acts 2:37) - causing radical change. The God that Jesus is describing is a God that is constantly desiring reconciliation, and he desires us to mimic that quality with one another.

It is because of empire's creation of justice *without* love that we insist on capital punishment; life in a dark prison cell; and perpetual war against others. It is because of empire's insistence of creating a justice *devoid* of love and compassion that we invented the doctrines and theologies of hell and an eternal punishment.

Jesus is telling us that we have to *love* our enemies. We cannot fully do that until we let go of what *we feel* is justice. We cannot fully do that until we learn to embrace the forgiveness, mercy, love, *and* justice of *God*.

Concerning Almsgiving

Jesus immediately follows the instruction for loving your enemies with a condemnation of false piety:

> "Beware of practicing your piety before
>
> others in order to be seen by them; for then
>
> you have no reward from your Father in
>
> heaven. So whenever you give alms, do not
>
> sound a trumpet before you, as the
>
> hypocrites do in the synagogues and in the
>
> streets, so that they may be praised by
>
> others. Truly I tell you, they have received

their reward. But when you give alms, do

not let your left hand know what your right

is doing, so that your alms may be done in

secret; and your Father who sees in secret

will reward you."[62]

If you can imagine a politician during election season who goes to a homeless shelter to get photographed and filmed by media outlets for handing out food, you get the picture of what Jesus was criticizing here.

Jesus is speaking directly against the corruption found in Jewish religious leaders who colluded with Rome for power and favor. These "leaders" would make grand gestures; pray loud and protracted prayers; and showboat their religious piety - all while enforcing rules of oppression and domination. Jesus uses the false piety of these religious elite as an example, and he warns his audience of the dangers of self-congratulatory "charity."

---

[62] Matthew 6:1-4

According to Jesus, the poor are blessed by God and should never be used or treated as a tool for self-aggrandizement. This type of self-righteous "charity," even if it is momentarily benefiting the poor and marginalized, ultimately demeans and devalues them because the "charity" is not intended for social uplift. It's intended for the benefit of the donor's stature and fame. Furthermore, if these leaders upheld a just society, charity would not be necessary in the first place.

Jesus instead directs his audience to give compassionately to those in need, and reminds us to do it without announcing it to everyone. Jesus tells them, "Your Father in heaven knows what you did," and so does the one you have been charitable to. Giving for the sake of goodness is its own reward. "Who are you doing this for?" we can hear Jesus asking. "Are you giving in order to receive adulation from the crowd, with your great charity, or are you caring for the least of these because you now understand that these are your sisters and brothers in God's unkingdom?"

"If you are giving in order to receive praise from the masses, you have already received your reward. However, if you are giving in order to love others in the way God has shown us to, then your reward will be great, for you have encountered God amongst the poor and vulnerable, and given to them out of love."

6
<u>THE RADICALITY OF THE LORD'S PRAYER</u>

Jesus follows his direction on giving with perhaps one of the most famous set of verses in the Christian Bible. The following passage is coined "The Lord's Prayer," where Jesus teaches his followers how to pray.

"And whenever you pray, do not be like the hypocrites; for they love to stand and pray in the synagogues and at the street corners, so that they may be seen by others. Truly I tell you, they have received their reward."

"When you are praying, do not heap up empty phrases as the Gentiles do; for they think that they will be heard because of their many words. Do not be like them, for your Father knows what you need before you ask him.

"Pray then in this way:

Our Father in heaven,

hallowed be your name.

Your kingdom come.

Your will be done,

on earth as it is in heaven.

Give us this day our daily bread.

And forgive us our debts,

as we also have forgiven our debtors.

And do not bring us to the time of trial,

but rescue us from the evil one.

For Yours is the kingdom and the power

and the glory forever. Amen.

For if you forgive others their trespasses,

your heavenly Father will also forgive you;

but if you do not forgive others, neither will

your Father forgive your trespasses."[63]

---

[63] Matthew 6:5-15

Throughout the centuries this prayer has been recited, quoted, and used in sermons. Sadly, it's radical nature, its *edge*, if you will, has been forgotten and hidden.

As we have already discussed, an oppressive empire ruled over the time and place that Jesus lived in. This empire's agenda was furthered by the religious elite in Judea through taxation, exploitation of the working class, and an enforcement of submission to "the powers that be." This coercion was all done under the guise of faith. The fact that Jesus challenged the authority structures of his day is extremely important in order to fully understand this prayer. Let's break down this prayer, one of the most powerful forms of protest, line by line.

The first line of Jesus' prayer reads:

> *"And whenever you pray, do not be like the hypocrites; for they love to stand and pray in the synagogues and at the street corners, so that they may be seen by others. Truly I tell you, they have received their reward."*

In this verse Jesus directly undermines the authorities and integrity of the religious leaders. Many of the Pharisees would congregate regularly in public spaces, where they would gather, making a great spectacle of their loud and vociferous prayer in front of crowds. As stated earlier, the Pharisees were well known for their knowledge and strict practice of religious code. It was in this strict adherence to the Law that religious authorities equated with piety. Jesus refutes this idea by saying, "don't be like them," calling them "hypocrites."[64]

The word "hypocrite" comes from the Greek word "*hypokrisis*," which means "to act out." It was mostly used when talking about actors who performed in plays. By calling these Pharisees "hypocrites," Jesus is saying that their practices and open prayer performances for the masses are not sincere. Jesus declares that the only reward the Pharisees will get from these "prayer plays" is the attention that they have *already* received from the multitudes that witnessed them praying aloud.

---

[64] Matthew 23:15

Jesus counters this practice by telling his listeners "whenever you pray, go into your room and shut the door and pray to your Father who is in secret; and your Father who sees in secret will reward you."[65]

According to Jesus, prayer is supposed to be an intimate act of conversation between yourself and God. Jesus tells his listeners that a genuine prayer does not require an audience to give approval or applause.

Again, Jesus issues a challenge:

> *"When you are praying, do not heap up empty phrases as the Gentiles do; for they think that they will be heard because of their many words. Do not be like them, for your Father knows what you need before you ask him."*

Jesus is saying that the point of prayer is not to present God with a wish list as if God were some sort of transcendental Santa Claus. Prayer is not about using eloquent words in the open for all

---

[65] Matthew 6:6

to hear and marvel at your piety. Prayer is about sharing your doubts, your fears, your disappointments, and your dreams with God. In turn, prayer is also about changing the reality and perception of the one praying so that they are more in tune with what God wants for the world and how their role helps make that desire possible.

Jesus is telling us that prayer does not only happen when we kneel beside our beds or pray aloud in front of peers. There is no official decree or stance you must make before you pray to your Eternal Parent. Rather, prayer can and should happen at all times. We should communicate with God throughout our day, no matter what we are doing.

Jesus then moves from explanation to example - from *doxis* to *praxis* - by teaching us a very specific prayer. This prayer is the one that we have taken to calling "The Lord's Prayer" throughout the centuries. As we look upon this prayer of Jesus, I will attempt to reveal its subversive nature in light of historical background and culture. The prayer begins in verse nine:

"Our Father in heaven, hallowed be your name."

This opening statement expresses Jesus' deep desire to retain the name of God as something holy. In Jesus' culture, and in some ways our own, a person's name also carried with it his or her reputation. Claiming you were a representative of someone meant that your actions would reflect upon them - so you were to act in a way that was worthy of the one you represented. For Jesus, to keep the name of God holy meant that we should act in a way that showed God's influence upon us, not just by what we say, (as Jesus accused the Pharisees of doing), but by what we do. Jesus was revealing that revering God's name, or by claiming that we are under God's influence, meant that it would reflect in how we lived; what we did for others and how we treated one another.

In verse ten, Jesus continues his prayer and begins his subversive remarks:

"your kingdom come, your will be done, on earth as it is in heaven."

This very statement is asking God's unkingdom to come and for his will to be done, as opposed to Caesar's kingdom and Caesar's will. Jesus' opening remarks reveal a rebellion against

Caesar and his empire. This empirical system, which oppresses and subjugates the poor and vulnerable, is what Jesus is speaking directly against. Jesus' prayer is asking God's unkingdom to eclipse Caesar's. For Jesus to call upon God's will to be done and God's unkingdom to "touch down" on all the earth means that he is praying for the empires, kingdoms, republics, nations, and governments that enslave and tyrannize its people to be uprooted and cast to the wind. The radical and defiant declaration that Jesus makes here is obvious. For the unkingdom of God to truly "touch down," and for God's will to fully exist here on earth means that the other kingdoms and empires, including the will of the Caesars, must cease to exist.

The revelation that Jesus is teaching us to call upon God's will and unkingdom in the here-and now flies in the face of much of our modern Western Christianity, which focuses on the "sweet by and by". In a Christianity that has turned its back on a hurting world while focusing itself on believing the "right things" to gain a ticket to heaven, the ideas and convictions of "God's unkingdom" and "God's will" become relegated to "another time in the future, in another place." However, if we read this passage correctly we can see Jesus pushing us to think of heaven in terms of being something tangible and in the here-and-now. He implies that heaven is something that is actively setting itself apart from the "powers and principalities" of this world right now and is inviting us all to join.

The next statement issues a challenge:

"Give us this day our daily bread."

To the poor and the destitute this prayer was good news. Jesus reveals a God who cares about the spiritual aspects of humanity and the physical condition. He reveals a God that desires for all of his/her children to be healthy, well, and full of joy. To those living in the margins of society, who struggled every day for their food, this was very good news.

However, to the wealthy and religious elite listening to Jesus' prayer, this statement was a provocation. Asking God for your "daily bread" was in stark contrast to receiving the abundance of food, wealth, comfort, and opulence that their lifestyles demanded. For the rich and powerful to ask God for mere "daily bread" challenged the notion of equating a successful life with the accumulation of wealth, fame, and power. This statement in Jesus' prayer was a declaration that all the food and riches the leaders and the ruling elite had stored up does not belong to them; it belongs to God, and God desires us to give it to everyone.

This portion of the prayer also ties back to Jewish Scripture, where Moses was leading his tribe of refugees from Egypt and into the "Promised Land." God provided food for the Israelites in the form of manna from heaven, and he instructed them to take only what they needed. When the Israelites attempted to take more than they needed and "store it up" for a later time, they would return to find the "manna" foul and full of worms. When the Israelites began to do what God had instructed, they found their food source clean and devoid of worms:

> Then the Lord said to Moses, 'I am going to
>
> rain bread from heaven for you, and each
>
> day the people shall go out and gather
>
> enough for that day. In that way I will test
>
> them, whether they will follow my
>
> instruction or not. On the sixth day, when

they prepare what they bring in, it will be twice as much as they gather on other days.'"

"…Moses said to them, 'It is the bread that the Lord has given you to eat. This is what the Lord has commanded: "Gather as much of it as each of you needs, an omer to a person according to the number of persons, all providing for those in their own tents."' The Israelites did so, some gathering more, some less. But when they measured it with an omer, those who gathered much had nothing over, and those who gathered little had no shortage; they gathered as much as each of them needed. …On the sixth day they gathered twice as much food, two omers apiece. When all the leaders of the congregation came and told Moses, he said to them, 'This is what the Lord has commanded: "Tomorrow is a day of solemn rest, a holy sabbath to the Lord; bake what

you want to bake and boil what you want to

boil, and all that is left over put aside to be

kept until morning.'" So they put it aside

until morning, as Moses commanded them;

and it did not become foul, and there were

no worms in it.[66]

The message from this passage in Exodus, which Jesus points to in his prayer, is that God desires that no one should pursue to store up treasure and wealth for themselves. He would rather have us work to ensure that no one goes without, and that we all have enough.

Jesus continues:

"And forgive us our debts, as we also have forgiven our debtors."

To live in the time of Jesus was to find yourself in a place of massive debt and inequality. The reality is that after Jerusalem and

---

[66] Exodus 16:1-24

its region became occupied by Rome, hefty taxes began to be levied and leaders who were loyal to Rome were appointed to collect them and "keep the peace." This created a shift in equality among the people. As it was earlier illustrated, farms and home settlements that had been passed down through families for generations were now being sold to pay for the taxes and the "kickbacks" to those who collected them. Former farm owners became day laborers who were now forced to work the fields that were formerly their own.

This unjust system created slavery through debt. This new serf class would become trapped in an endless cycle of poverty due to ever-increasing debt and taxation; struggling to pay for the necessities of life for themselves and their families.

As a result of the massive debt that this poor working-class could not repay, a form of slavery was instituted. The one in debt would work off their debt in servitude to the debtor until all was repaid in full. But here's the catch. The more you worked to pay off your debt, the more you would owe. Your housing, the food you and your family would consume, the clothes that you would wear - this would all be rolled in to the continuous cycle of debt as you worked to repay what was originally owed. As a result of this oppressive system, your servitude was guaranteed to be passed on to your children.

Jesus saw that debt and servitude were new ways for Roman powers and the religious elite to control the populace. Jesus words his prayer beautifully:

"...forgive us our debts, as we have also forgiven our debtors."

Jesus tells his audience that the way things currently are is not the way things should be. By framing the argument of debt in a way that reveals that "everyone owes something to somebody," Jesus flips the system upside down and demands that those who wish to be forgiven of even small debts should first forgive the debts owed to them. This new economic ideal is one where forgiveness and mercy are the currencies rather than competitions of greed and unjust compensation. This conviction comes through Jesus' understanding of the Year of Jubilee, which I contend is what Jesus viewed as the prototype for God's unkingdom on this earth.

The Year of Jubilee, found in the books of Leviticus and Deuteronomy, called for a redistribution of wealth and property.

According to these texts, land and all wealth belonged to God, and God allowed this land and wealth to be used by all that dwell in this world, not as owners, but as custodians who were to utilize it as a common treasury for all. Every forty-nine years all of this land and wealth was to be returned to God and to be redistributed so that none would go without.[67]

> *"In this year of Jubilee you shall return, every one of you, to your property" (Leviticus 25:13).*

In the Year of Jubilee, all debts would be canceled and forgotten and all debt-slaves would be set free.

> *"Every seventh year you shall grant a remission of debts" (Deuteronomy 15:1).*

> *"Then they and their children with them shall be free from your authority; they shall go back to their own family and return to their ancestral property" (Leviticus 25:41).*

---

[67] Leviticus 25:13-55

Finally, the Year of Jubilee was a celebration and a holy vacation. The land that was used for farming was given a rest, along with all who till it.

> *"That fiftieth year shall be a jubilee for you: you shall not sow, or reap the aftergrowth, or harvest the unpruned vines. For it is a jubilee; it shall be holy to you: you shall eat only what the field itself produces."*
> *(Leviticus 25:11-12).*

It matters not what empire or republic, nor what time period one finds themselves in. Declaring that Caesar's crown or the President's White House doesn't belong to them, but instead must be handed over to the poor, are words that will bring great comfort to the oppressed and impoverished, but will also cause great distress and ire among the wealthy and powerful. So may it always be.

Jesus then moves into temptation:

> *"And lead us not into temptation,*
>
> *But deliver us from the evil one.*

When Jesus teaches his audience to ask not to be led into temptation and instead to be delivered from the evil one, he is revealing that God is the one who leads followers down the paths of mercy, righteousness, love, and justice. When examining this passage with the rest of the meaning behind this prayer, we discover Jesus feels that following God's will and becoming citizens of God's unkingdom will deliver us from evil, a path that would seek to tempt us to seek wealth and power, which results in forsaking the poor and oppressed.

Jesus ends his prayer where he began, with a subversive and rebellious nature:

"For Yours is the kingdom and the power and the glory forever.

Amen."

Jesus declares that God's unkingdom, power, and glory overshadow and will overthrow the kingdoms, powers, and glories demanded by Caesar. "The throne Caesar sits upon" we can hear Jesus saying, "It belongs to the God of love and justice." Jesus, again, is revealing that the unkingdom of God, in all it's beauty, justice, equality, and love, is everything that the empires and kingdoms of this world are not.

Jesus ends this radical prayer with a message on forgiveness:

> *"For if you forgive others their trespasses, your heavenly Father will also forgive you; but if you do not forgive others, neither will your Father forgive your trespasses."*

To be under the "boot" of an unjust system is to feel helpless, hopeless, and rage. Jesus reveals that another world is not only possible, it has come. He shares that in order to seek reconciliation, one must let go of their hatred. To experience the love of God, who freely gives this love, Jesus tells his hearers they must let go of the feelings of retribution and vengeance towards those in power. Jesus realized that holding onto fantasies of revenge would lead to a life unfulfilled. Refusing to forgive one who has purposefully wronged you matters not to the offender. Actively forgiving releases you as much as it releases the wrongdoer. Refusing to forgive that person, holding onto that anger and hatred, is akin to poisoning yourself, fully expecting it to kill the guilty party.

Furthermore, how can you expect to be forgiven for your wrongs if you are unwilling to forgive those who have wronged you?

7
<u>FAUX DEVOTION & REDISTRIBUTION OF WEALTH</u>

As Jesus closes on his teachings about prayer, he again touches on the issue of outward piety and false righteousness. This time, the issue is fasting:

> "And whenever you fast, do not look
>
> dismal, like the hypocrites, for they disfigure
>
> their faces so as to show others that they are
>
> fasting. Truly I tell you, they have received
>
> their reward. But when you fast, put oil on
>
> your head and wash your face, so that your
>
> fasting may be seen not by others but by
>
> your Father who is in secret; and your
>
> Father who sees in secret will reward you."

The act of fasting is deeply tied into social justice and renewal. The prophet Isaiah declared this in his writings:

> "Is not this the fast that I choose:
>
> to loose the bonds of injustice,

to undo the thongs of the yoke,

to let the oppressed go free,

and to break every yoke?

Is it not to share your bread with the

hungry,

and bring the homeless poor into your

house;

when you see the naked, to cover them,

and not to hide yourself from your own

kin?

Then your light shall break forth like the

dawn,

and your healing shall spring up quickly;

your vindicator shall go before you,

the glory of the LORD shall be your rear

guard.

Then you shall call, and the LORD will

answer;

you shall cry for help, and he will say, Here

I am."[68]

Jesus, who took many of his cues from prophetic writings, also saw fasting to be something to bring about justice. It must have infuriated Jesus to witness the religious leaders reveal to the populace that they were fasting by making themselves look disheveled and in pain from hunger, all in order to gain applause and approval for their outward holiness.

Jesus tells his audience, "Who are you doing this for? If it's for God, why go out of your way to reveal to others that you're doing it? Don't be like the religious elite who feign religious piety and great faith while in front of large crowds. Because, behind closed doors, these same men work with Caesar to cheat you out of your property and pay. Don't be like them. When you fast, fast for the right reasons - seek to fast to call on God's unkingdom for the justice and equality of all people."

Concerning Treasures, The Sound Eye, and Serving Two Masters

---

[68] Isaiah 58:6-8

Jesus moves from his instruction on prayer into his direction on property and accumulation of wealth:

"Do not store up for yourselves treasures on earth, where moth and rust consume and where thieves break in and steal; but store up for yourselves treasures in heaven, where neither moth nor rust consumes and where thieves do not break in and steal. For where your treasure is, there your heart will be also."

"The eye is the lamp of the body. So, if your eye is healthy, your whole body will be full of light; but if your eye is unhealthy, your whole body will be full of darkness. If then the light in you is darkness, how great is the darkness.

"No one can serve two masters; for a slave will either hate the one and love the other, or be devoted to the one and despise the

other. You cannot serve God and wealth."[69]

These three sections, which are separated in most modern biblical translations, are here placed together intentionally, as they all coincide with one another. Jesus reveals that an accumulation of wealth and a focus on private property over the needs of others blinds us and "snuffs" out the light within us. Once this light is extinguished from the pursuit of "stuff," we feel empty and attempt to fill the void with more wealth, property, and treasure. This is not the way of the unkingdom of God. We must choose our master - God or Mammon.

Simply put, Jesus saw private property and the accumulation of wealth as theft against the poor and vulnerable. We can hear Jesus say: "Brothers and sisters," we can hear Jesus say, "do not store up for yourselves riches you will never need; that belongs to others so that they can live a happy and healthy life. For if you choose your power, your wealth, and your property over God, your light, the

---

[69] Matthew 6:19-24

spark of creation, will be snuffed out from within you and replaced

by a darkness until you come to your senses."

There is no better example in our modern times than that of

Founder and CEO of Amazon.com, Jeff Bezos – the richest man in

the world. While he is estimated to be worth $143.1 billion, his

factory employee tell horror stories of poor working conditions and

living off of State Welfare.[70]

The idea of private property, as we have become accustomed

to understanding it, was in large part invented by the Romans a

little over a century before Jesus entered the scene. This idea of

private property encompassed anything a Roman citizen might own

- including a slave - and reduced them to chattel that is owned. The

basic premise of property in the legal sense of Roman law was

concerned with the relationship between the owner and an item. Is

it a "possession," meaning that one has control of a specific good

or service? Or is it "property," meaning that one has absolute legal

title and control over something?

---

[70] https://www.businessinsider.com/amazon-warehouse-workers-share-their-horror-stories-2018-4

Wealth in Jesus' time, just like in our day, was only mass accumulated through the manipulation, coercion, theft, and the metaphorical stepping on the backs of others. This accumulation of things and hoarding of mass wealth, which most definitely included land deeds and housing, inevitably left countless numbers of people in homelessness, debt, and poverty. It is to this that Jesus sought to turn the whole of society on its ear.

Seeing Jesus' statements regarding the accumulation of wealth in this light reveals to us the questions being asked in between the lines:

> Why is the landlord charging you a week's wage in order for you and your family to reside at one of his property homes? Is he using it? Doesn't he have his own place to sleep and live? That's a beautiful mosaic tile you paid a small fortune to purchase and then paid 8 men a slave's wage to to install; what good is it? Can you use it? Does it serve a purpose other than to elevate your

status? Couldn't that money, instead, have gone into better use by serving the poor and vulnerable? Your banquet feasts are fantastic! There are rows upon rows of food and the wine glass is never empty. Why did you choose to spend this feast with those who already are capable of affording their own feast? Why did you not, instead, invite your poor neighbor?

To Jesus, this accumulation of private property and wealth is theft. "You chose to stockpile your riches and treasures here at the expense of others. The true treasure in God's unkingdom is service to others and living with all things in common with one another. Your wealth has blinded you and extinguished your light, and now you stumble blindly in the dark, insisting that more possessions and riches will guide your path. You have chosen your deity, and it is not God."

This conviction carried into the first Jesus-centered assemblies and congregations. According to *The Acts of the*

Apostles, the earliest churches "were together and had all things in common; they would sell their possessions and goods and distribute the proceeds to all, as any had need... those who believed were of one heart and soul, and no one claimed private ownership of possessions, but everything they owned was held in common."[71]

This understanding of Jesus' message continued well into the 2nd Century as well, as is evidenced by the writings of the Early Church Father, Justin Martyr, who declared: "We who once took most pleasure in the means of increasing our wealth and property now bring what we have into a common fund and share with everyone in need."[72] Clement of Alexandria (150-215 CE) followed suit in writing that "Private property is the fruit of iniquity. I know that God has given us the use of goods, but only as far as is necessary; and he has determined that the use shall be common. The use of all things that are found in this world ought to be common to all men. Only the most manifest iniquity makes one say to another, 'This belongs

---

[71] Acts 2:44-45; 4:32

[72] Justin Martyr, *First Apology*, 14

to me, that to you.' Hence the origin of contention among men."[73] Even the writers outside of the Early Church saw the Jesus-followers' refusal of private property and spoke of it, declaring that "Christians despise all possessions and share them mutually."[74]

The message of Jesus in the passages is clear: Accumulating wealth and treasures is incompatible with God's unkingdom. The Bezos, Bushs, Trumps, Buffetts, Clintons, and Musks of this world have been warned!

---

[73] Clement of Alexandria, *Paedagogus*,2

[74] Lucian of Samosata, *Peregrinus*, 13

8
<u>THE NEW COMMUNITY</u>

I remember serving some of our homeless friends in North Georgia a few years back one Sunday morning. One of the guys we served came up with a t-shirt that read: "Some People Are So Poor, All They Have Is Money". That statement really struck me, as the accumulation of power and wealth stem from a most basic fear of never having enough.

Many interpret the following passage as Jesus bringing comfort to the poor, that they should not concern themselves with the essentials of life and that God will provide for them. While this line of thought has merit in this passage, I believe Jesus is digging deeper - especially in relation to the passages that preceded it.

"Therefore I tell you, do not worry about

your life, what you will eat or what you will

drink, or about your body, what you will

wear. Is not life more than food, and the

body more than clothing? Look at the birds

of the air; they neither sow nor reap nor

gather into barns, and yet your heavenly

Father feeds them. Are you not of more value than they? And can any of you by worrying add a single hour to your span of life? And why do you worry about clothing? Consider the lilies of the field, how they grow; they neither toil nor spin, yet I tell you, even Solomon in all his glory was not clothed like one of these. But if God so clothes the grass of the field, which is alive today and tomorrow is thrown into the oven, will he not much more clothe you—you of little faith? Therefore do not worry, saying, 'What will we eat?' or 'What will we drink?' or 'What will we wear?' For it is the Gentiles who strive for all these things; and indeed your heavenly Father knows that you need all these things. But strive first for the kingdom of God and his righteousness, and all these things will be given to you as well.

"So do not worry about tomorrow, for

tomorrow will bring worries of its own.

Today's trouble is enough for today."[75]

Jesus is immediately following up his instructions against

accumulating wealth and private property by striking at the heart of

social inequality: fear.

Jesus asks his listeners. "Why do you concern yourself so

deeply about what you will have to eat?" Jesus saw that this worry,

this fear, leads one to stockpile food in excess to where others have

not. "Does not God provide for the birds of the air? Fear not."

Jesus continues, "Why are you so afraid of what clothes you

will wear? Is not the body more than clothes?" This concern of

clothing options reveals that Jesus is not merely addressing the

poor among his listeners, who relied on their own craftmanship to

make their clothing. Jesus again is revealing how fear, this time

towards one's outward appearances, causes the stockpiling of

excess; spending your riches upon many articles of clothing while

the poor and vulnerable remain dressed in "rags." "Do not the

---

[75] Matt. 6:25-34

flowers in the field wear more beautiful colors than even King Solomon? Fear not."

Jesus counters the predominant desire to accumulate wealth, and to stockpile essentials with the simplicity of life found in God's unkingdom:

> "...your heavenly Father knows that you need all these things. But strive first for the kingdom of God and his righteousness, and all these things will be given to you as well."

Jesus reveals that if we abandon empire and its notions of power, wealth, and fame, we can see that God has already provided all one needs to sustain life and live happily in harmony with one another. Again, Jesus is pointing to an abandonment of private property, of sharing all things in common, and creating a common treasury for all. In doing so, Jesus saw that none would go without and that all would prosper.

<u>Judging Others</u>

"Do not judge, so that you may not be

judged. For with the judgment you make

you will be judged, and the measure you give

will be the measure you get. Why do you see

the speck in your neighbor's eye, but do not

notice the log in your own eye? Or how can

you say to your neighbour, 'Let me take the

speck out of your eye', while the log is in

your own eye? You hypocrite, first take the

log out of your own eye, and then you will

see clearly to take the speck out of your

neighbor's eye."[76]

Another two-dimensional declaration is brought into the audience's midst as Jesus condemns the action of a human judging another human. While this speaks very much to the individual interactions between two citizens within God's unkingdom, Jesus is also speaking to the powers of empire. Jesus reveals the hypocritical actions of empire that pass judgment against the poor while it

---

[76] Matt. 7:1-5

commits the same heinous acts in excess. We can draw a parallel from this section to Jesus' earlier instruction on non-violent resistance, specifically where he describes a man being sued for his coat.[77] In this instance, his words are to the elite and the empirical system that supports them, who would hold tribunals and legal cases against others. When viewed in this light, these words against judgment take on an even greater meaning.

How many governmental courts have condemned a man to die for murder while committing mass murder through war? How many governmental courts have tried and convicted others of theft while empire has created economic systems that steal the land, the riches, and the prosperity of the many and place them into the hands of a few? How can a court condemn men for trespass when the empire invaded an occupied land and called it their own? Jesus demands an answer! How dare you condemn a man for the speck of sawdust in their eye while you have an entire log in your own? Remove your log, dismantle your systems of injustice and only then dare to speak of the man who has merely sawdust in his eye. Seek

---

[77] Matt. 5:40

reconciliation and forgiveness. This is the only way in the unkingdom of God.

<u>Profaning the Holy</u>

> "Do not give what is holy to dogs; and do
> not throw your pearls before swine, or they
> will trample them under foot and turn and
> maul you."[78]

The explanations for this verse have many wide and varied theories. We would do a great disservice to scholarship and authentic faith if we did not point out the most obvious and most uncomfortable understanding.

Jesus tells his audience not to give what is holy to "dogs." Dogs, in Jesus' time, were not seen as the family pet that we know and love today. Dogs throughout the Roman Empire and Provinces were mostly wild and roamed the outskirts of civilization in packs. When you imagine a wild animal pack sharing a meal, your mind does not visualize anything pretty. Whatever the pack had caught to

---

[78] Matthew 7:6

eat is utterly decimated and ripped apart. Jesus is telling his hearers not to toss away God's unkingdom and what God declares as sacred - love, community, relationship, leaving those sacred things to the wild dogs.

"Swine" as we know are unclean animals that violate Kosher Law in Jewish practice, but were an animal well-loved for consumption by the Gentiles, which was used as an insult by the Jewish people towards the Roman Empire. In this light, we see that Jesus could be telling his audience that one shouldn't attempt to appease the Roman Empire with precious things like loyalty and fealty. Like a group of wild hogs, when the Empire finds that it cannot consume such things, it will take its armies and destroy them.

Ask, Search, Knock

> "Ask, and it will be given to you; search, and
> you will find; knock, and the door will be
> opened for you. For everyone who asks
> receives, and everyone who searches finds,
> and for everyone who knocks, the door will

be opened. Is there anyone among you who,

if your child asks for bread, will give a

stone? Or if the child asks for a fish, will

give a snake? If you then, who are evil,

know how to give good gifts to your

children, how much more will your Father

in heaven give good things to those who ask

him!"[79]

Jesus reinforces the idea that the unkingdom of God is a family, with God as the loving and compassionate Parent. Perhaps this section of Jesus' sermon should be named "The Eternal Parent's Example." The God that Jesus describes is one of great generosity, happily giving what is needed to her children who ask. The focus for Jesus in this section is not so much the request asked of God. Rather, it is revealing that God is gracious in his giving, withholding nothing from her children. This radical nature of giving is in stark contrast to the empires and kingdoms of this

---

[79] Matthew 7:7-11

world, whose leaders and Caesars seek to withhold the lion's share

for themselves, leaving the huddled masses to fight for the scraps.

9

THE PATH TOWARDS A JUST SOCIETY

Jesus follows up his description of God and God's gracious nature with instruction on how God's children should respond to such radical generosity:

> "In everything do to others as you would
>
> have them do to you; for this is the law and
>
> the prophets."[80]

Jesus' instruction to "do unto others" follows in line with the rabbinical school of Hillel, which roughly 100 years before Jesus, declared: "Do not do to others what you would not have them do to you."[81] Jesus, in his radical fashion, points to the great rabbi's teaching and reveals the importance of love within this new community - this new unkingdom of God. Loving without distinction of neighbor - no longer worrying about who is "in" and who is "out" - is of vital importance to the message of Jesus and his conviction of God's unkingdom. Jesus brings the message full-

---

[80] Matthew 7:12

[81] Shabbat 31a

circle by declaring that this way of radical love, in freely giving as God has given to us all, the Law and the words of the Prophets is fulfilled.

How does this "Golden Rule" - these sets of ethics shared by Jesus that reveal a God of radical hospitality and generosity, as well as and a citizenry dedicated to doing to others what they would have done to them - compare when contrasted with the empires of this world? These governments that were created and sustained by their uses of force, yet condemn and murder a man for using force against it, cannot abide by this "Golden Rule". The empires of this world cannot even abide by their own laws, much less follow the ethics set forth by God's unkingdom.

"...do to others as you would have them to to you."

Do you not wish to be condemned to poverty by the elite minority that amasses wealth for themselves? Then do not condemn others to poverty.

Do you wish not to be ruled and subjugated by others? Then do not rule and subjugate.

Do to others as you would have them do to you.

The Narrow Gate

> "Enter through the narrow gate; for the gate
>
> is wide and the road is easy that leads to
>
> destruction, and there are many who take it.
>
> For the gate is narrow and the road is hard
>
> that leads to life, and there are few who find
>
> it."[82]

The Narrow Gate. This statement by Jesus, (along with many others, as we've seen) has also lost its radical meaning. The majority of churches, even those outside the church, have come to understand this statement as nothing more than believing in Jesus, and all the "right" things about him, so that you can go to heaven when you die. *Right* practices. *Proper* rituals. *Right* beliefs. What cruel twist of fate would have the words of Jesus distorted to mean the exact opposite of what he was attempting to get across?

---

[82] Matthew 7:13-14

The "narrow gate" that Jesus speaks of is actually his teachings and examples. As revealed throughout this sermon, Jesus is not interested in if his hearers can perfect the rituals that the pious religious elite perform. Jesus is not concerned with whether or not his audience has their theology measured out in a straight, discernible line. Jesus does not care if this crowd simply claims they *believe* in him. Jesus wants your heart; for where your treasure is, your heart will also be. The narrow gate is difficult to find and even more difficult to walk through because it requires actual practice. To discover this path, his followers have to *actually* love their enemies, turn the other cheek, seek to reject violence, reject the notions of revenge, and abandon their riches, property, and treasure. To walk this path between the narrow gate, Jesus tells his hearers that you have to actually put faith in God's unkingdom and its path into action.

This theme remains in play through the next two sections of Jesus' sermon, warning his audience of those who would lead them astray from God's unkingdom, as well as cautioning them of what is required in order to claim citizenship in this beautiful unkingdom.

"Beware of false prophets, who come to you in sheep's clothing but inwardly are ravenous wolves. You will know them by their fruits. Are grapes gathered from thorns, or figs from thistles? In the same way, every good tree bears good fruit, but the bad tree bears bad fruit. A good tree cannot bear bad fruit, nor can a bad tree bear good fruit. Every tree that does not bear good fruit is cut down and thrown into the fire. Thus you will know them by their fruits."[83]

Jesus has spent a great deal in this sermon on pointing out the hypocrisy of the religious elite who had colluded with Rome. The false piety of the politician/priest is easy to identify and Jesus reveals, in great detail, that their master is power, wealth, and fame.

---

[83] Matthew 7:15-20

In this passage, Jesus is also referring to a different group - the Zealots.

The Zealots of Jesus' time were a political group of rebels that worked within the Judean Province, inciting violence against their Roman oppressors in an attempt to overthrow the Empire from the Holy Land. Founded in 6 BCE, these Zealots, along with the factions that were created through them, would disrupt the populace with violence. They would assault those they deemed were "conspiring with Rome" and engage in all-out warfare during the revolt against Herod Agrippa II. To Jesus, these rebels that sought to overthrow an oppressive regime were the blades and the "fire" that were actively cutting down and burning the "bad fruit" produced by oppressive and empirical rule.

Jesus declares: "You will know them by their fruits."

Jesus is asking his audience not to be fooled by those who he deemed "false prophets" – priests of the establishment who have their lofty positions due to their fealty to Rome. Passive violence – be it through supporting policies that keep others poor and impoverished, approving of war, police brutality, and mass incarceration, and creating societies where the poor and oppressed cannot get their basic needs met – is still a form of sadistic violence. Jesus is warning the establishment leaders that they are trees that bear bad fruit and that they will be revealed for what they are. When they do they will be cut down and cast aside like other rubbish to be burned.

Concerning Self-Deception

> "Not everyone who says to me, 'Lord, Lord', will enter the kingdom of heaven, but only one who does the will of my Father in heaven. On that day many will say to me, 'Lord, Lord, did we not prophesy in your name, and cast out demons in your name, and do many deeds of power in your name?' Then I will declare to them, 'I never knew you; go away from me, you evildoers.'"[84]

After warning against false prophets, Jesus moves his focus back to the religious elite. The smooth-talking, wealthy priests who

---

[84] Matthew 7:21-23

actively colluded with Rome continually evoked the name of God, crying "Lord, Lord" with such apparent passion and sincerity. Yet through their actions, they refuse to follow the way of God's unkingdom. Jesus reveals that talk is cheap. If one claims to follow God, it will be revealed by what they do for the poor and vulnerable. Jesus saw that using words to claim you represented God and "the least of these"[85] while working to oppress and exploit them was one of the worst sins one could commit.

Jesus declared that "On that day that God touches down, fully revealing her unkingdom, those that use these eloquent words and practice fake piety will be revealed for what they are: charlatans." On that day, Jesus reveals, these charlatans will attempt to gain God's attention by stating "We evoked your name openly every day! We cast out demons in your name! We did things many things in power using your name!" Jesus shares that on that day, God will respond:

"You claim that you called my name continually. You claim that you gave me credit for the power you amassed and actions you

---

[85] Matthew 25:31-46

made. If you called out to me, why did I not hear you? Are you sure you were not actually uttering your own name so that you could elevate yourself? You think you know me, but you don't. Depart from me and those you have harmed with your word and deed until you figure out who I am and what my unkingdom is truly about."

10
<u>HEARING AND DOING</u>

As we come to the close of Jesus' sermon, (and this book), I want to ask again: What if Jesus meant all those things he said? What would the Church look like if we took Jesus' words seriously? Not just the Church, but what would the world look like? The Trumps and Rockefellers of the world would go away empty-handed. The racist forces that make up ICE and police departments would disband. The Richard Spencers and Alex Joneses of the world would issue an apology and quickly beg for forgiveness. This is but a snippet of what acting on Jesus' message would look like.

> "Everyone then who hears these words of mine and acts on them will be like a wise man who built his house on rock. The rain fell, the floods came, and the winds blew and beat on that house, but it did not fall, because it had been founded on rock. And everyone who hears these words of mine and does not act on them will be like a

foolish man who built his house on sand.

The rain fell, and the floods came, and the

winds blew and beat against that house, and

it fell—and great was its fall!

"Now when Jesus had finished saying these

things, the crowds were astounded at his

teaching, for he taught them as one having

authority, and not as their scribes."[86]

Jesus closes his sermon with a radical indictment against the

powers and principalities of this world. "Have you heard my words

today?" Jesus asks his audience. "This empire - this way of *doing*

that has oppressed, murdered, and destroyed the beautiful world

that our Parent has created - it's a sinking ship whose Captain will

go down with it, and lock up all of the ship's passengers in their

barracks so that they too go down with him."

Jesus continues: "Do not build your 'house' - stake your way of

life - on the shaky ground that is empire. Empire, because of its use

of violence and force - its oppression and injustice - makes the

---

86 Matthew 7:24-29

ground underneath it loose like sand and will crumble under the weight of itself at the first sign of rain by a greater empire or power. Instead, build your life upon something solid. These teachings, like the rock foundation you have built your 'house' upon, are hard, but once embraced can withstand any storm the powers and principalities can churn against you. Don't just let this message go in one ear and out the other - embrace it; live it out! It is the path to God's unkingdom; it is the path to equality, love, and justice."

We all know how this story for Jesus ends. This anti-imperial message eventually finds Jesus tried, beaten, and executed on a Roman cross as an insurrectionist to the State. However, the Jesus-movement continued.

As we have discovered, the Early Church took Jesus' message to heart:

> "All who believed were together and had
> things in common; they would sell their
> possessions and goods and distribute the
> proceeds to all, as any had need. Day by day,
> as they spent time together in the temple,

they broke bread at home and ate their food

with glad and generous hearts, praising God

and having the goodwill of all the people.

Now the whole group of those who believed

were of one heart and soul, and no one

claimed private ownership of any

possessions, but everything they owned was

held in common... There was not a needy

person among them, for as many as owned

lands or houses sold them and brought the

proceeds of what was sold. They laid it at

the apostles' feet, and it was distributed to

each as any had need."[87]

In the pre-Constantinian Early Church, we saw that conviction of compassion towards the sick and the poor was carried out even when plague and famine sacked Rome. When the rest of the Roman populace fled the plague, the early band of Jesus followers stayed behind to care for the sick and impoverished.

---

[87] Acts 2:44-46; 4:32, 34-35

"All day long some of them tended to the

dying and to their burial, countless numbers

with no one to care for them. Others

gathered together from all parts of the city a

multitude of those withered from famine

and distributed bread to them all."[88]

This generosity of spirit and this adherence to the unkingdom of God even gave Caesar pause:

"...when it came about that the poor were

neglected and overlooked by the priests,

then I think the impious Galileans [Jesus-

followers] observed this fact and devoted

themselves to philanthropy... They support

not only their poor but ours as well, all men

see that our people lack aid from us."[89]

Was this not Jesus' intention? Jesus' vision of God's unkingdom saw that the actions and words of this unkingdom's

---

[88] Eusebius, *The Church History* (Grand Rapids: Kregel, 2007), 293.

[89] Emperor Julian, *Letter to a Priest* and *To Arsacius*

citizens would reveal themselves to be so irresistible that even the Caesars of this world would be incapable of resisting, abandoning their thrones and repenting of their sins so that they could join the sacred community.

And what about us? Empires and Caesars still claim dominion over this world. Even worse, many of these empires have claimed adherence to Jesus' message in order to conquer and dominate others. Since the time of Emperor Constantine, the majority of Christianity - the followers of Jesus - have been co-opted by empire, serving it and twisting the words of their teacher to serve their worldly masters.

How can this be changed? How can we return to seeing the radical message that Jesus laid forth - the one his earliest followers adopted and practiced - a way that even gave a Caesar pause? It is my contention that those of us with ears to hear, eyes to see, and minds to think must reclaim this radical message of Jesus. We must take it back from the imposters who have turned Jesus into a "meek and mild" person who spoke of merely moral platitudes, taught his followers that "right belief" was all that mattered, and demanded that we focus solely on a sweet afterlife. These radical words must be taken out of the modern Church, whose four-walled institution has held Jesus' message captive and prevented it from challenging anything of worth. These words of Jesus must be snatched away from those who seek to tame the Lion of Judah - who desire Jesus solely for a "ticket to heaven" - and returned to the huddled masses; the ones that Jesus called upon us to serve. For the gospel is truly "good news," but that news is only good when it is utilized and practiced for its intended purposes, which are to turn the whole world upside down. To dismantle the empires and systems of oppression brick by brick. To create a beloved community of love, equality, justice, and joy. This is the unkingdom of God Jesus pointed us to. This is the message of Jesus' Sermon on the Mount. The question is, now that you've heard the message, what will you do with it? As Saint Maria of Paris once stated, "Christianity is either fire or it is nothing." May we be the spark that ignites the revolution of love and change.

The End